International Logistics

HIGHER NATIONAL DIPLOMA

国际物流

【英】苏格兰学历管理委员会（SQA）

英文原版

Unit Student Guide

BUSINESS

D4X8 35

中国时代经济出版社

SCOTTISH QUALIFICATIONS AUTHORITY

China Modern Economic Publishing House

International Logistics
Unit Student Guide

Contents

1 Introduction to the unit · 1

    1.1   Outcomes · 1
    1.2   Unit structure · 2
    1.3   How to use these learning materials · 2
    1.4   Symbols used in this unit · 3

2 Other resources required · 7

3 Assessment information · 9

    3.1   How you will be assessed · 9
    3.2   When and where you will be assessed · 9
    3.3   What you have to achieve · 10
    3.4   Opportunities for reassessment · 10

4 Section 1: Systems approach to organisations · 11

    4.1   Introduction to this section · 11
    4.2   Assessment information for this section · 12
    4.3   Elements of an international logistics system · 13
    4.4   Globalisation · 18
    4.5   Logistics··· what is it? · 36

©Scottish Qualifications Authority 2004

4.6	Strategic and operational planning	43
4.7	Economic factors	54
4.8	Summary of this section	65
4.9	Answers to SAQs	66
4.10	Answers to activities	70
4.11	Case study	71

5   Section 2: The importance of customer service   73

5.1	Introduction to this section	73
5.2	Assessment information for this section	75
5.3	Elements of customer service	77
5.4	Summary of this section	115
5.5	Answers to SAQs	116
5.6	Answers to activities	119

6   Section 3: Operation of the major components of an international logistics network   123

6.1	Introduction to this section	123
6.2	Assessment information for this section	124
6.3	Logistics decisions: elements of the logistics network	125
6.4	Summary of this section	183
6.5	Answers to SAQs	184
6.6	Answers to activities	189

7   Section 4: Range of services provided   193

7.1	Introduction to this section	193
7.2	Assessment information for this section	194
7.3	Services provided by international logistics firms	195

7.4	On the move	205
7.5	In-house provision and outsourcing	215
7.6	Outsourcing logistics services	215
7.7	Location of companies	221
7.8	Representation for freight forwarders	221
7.9	Marketing plans	222
7.10	Summary of this section	226
7.11	Answers to SAQs	229

8 Section 5: Forces of change and future developments 231

8.1	Introduction to this section	231
8.2	Assessment information for this section	232
8.3	Change impacting on the future development of international logistics	233
8.4	Electronic data interchange	233
8.5	Reverse logistics	249
8.6	Current issues concerning green logistics in the logistics industry	283
8.7	Supply chain issues for the future of international logistics	292
8.8	Summary of this section	297
8.9	Answers to SAQs	299
8.10	Answers to activities	302

9 Glossary 305

10 Acknowledgements 307

1 Introduction to the unit

This unit is written to enable candidates to recognise the individual elements of logistics and to understand how effective integration of these maximises corporate performance as well as seeing the ways in which logistics impacts other corporate functions.

The unit is aimed at those who have some prior knowledge of the major business functions.

Access is at the discretion of the centre.

1.1 Outcomes

There are five outcomes:

1. Explain the systems approach to organisations in the context of the logistics activity.

2. Assess the importance of customer service to the provision of a competitive logistics and distribution strategy.

3. Describe the operation of the major components of an international logistics network.

4. Examine the range of services provided by international logistics businesses.

5. Assess the forces for change impacting the future development of international logistics.

1.2 Unit structure

This unit contains the following study sections:

Section number and title		Approx. study time
1	Systems approach to organisations	12 hours
2	Importance of customer service	12 hours
3	Operation of major components	12 hours
4	Range of services provided	12 hours
5	Change impacting future development	12 hours

1.3 How to use these learning materials

The materials should be used as base for discussion and learning. Most of the main points required to be addressed in the unit will be included in the materials. However, candidates will be expected to read more extensively and research aspects/operations within the industry. This is a very diverse industry and change takes place all the time. A good source of up-to-date information will be found in newspapers and the annual reports of some of the large logistics operators. The materials cover the breadth of provision within the logistics industry and do not follow the operation of any one single company or group of companies.

1.4 Symbols used in this unit

These learning materials allow you to work on your own with tutor support. As you work through the course, you will encounter a series of symbols which indicate that something follows that you are expected to do. You will notice that as you work through the study sections you will be asked to undertake a series of self-assessed questions, activities and tutor assignments. An explanation of the symbols used to identify these is given below.

Self-Assessed Question

This symbol is used to indicate a self-assessed question (SAQ). Most commonly, SAQs are used to check your understanding of the material that has already been covered in the sections.

This type of assessment is self contained; everything is provided within the section to enable you to check your understanding of the materials.

The process is simple:

- you are set SAQs throughout the study section;

- you respond to these by writing either in the space provided in the assessment itself or in your notebook;

- on completion of the SAQ, you turn to the back of the section to compare the model SAQ answers to your own;

- if you are not satisfied after checking your responses, turn to the appropriate part of the study section and go over the topic again.

Remember — the answers to SAQs are contained within the study materials. You are not expected to guess at these answers.

Activity

 1

This symbol indicates an activity, which is normally a task you will be asked to do that should improve or consolidate your understanding of the subject in general or a particular feature of it.

The suggested responses to activities are given at the end of each section.

Remember that the SAQs and activities contained within your package are intended to allow you to check your understanding and monitor your own progress throughout the course. It goes without saying that the answers to these should only be checked after the SAQ or activity has been completed. If you refer to these answers before completing the SAQs or activities, you cannot expect to get maximum benefit from your course.

International Logistics
Unit Student Guide

China Modern Economic Publishing House

Tutor assignment — formative assignment

This symbol means that a tutor assignment follows. These are found at the end of each study section. The aim of the tutor assignment is to cover and/or incorporate the main topics of the section and prepare you for unit (summative) outcome assessment. In this guide all assessments centre around a case study scenario augmented by further reading and/or research. The actual case study scenario is included at the end of Section 1 with assessment questions included at the end of each study section, as appropriate.

2 Other resources required

As stated above candidates will be expected to read and research. It would be advisable to have access to the Internet, magazines and newspapers. No other resources are required but may be provided at the discretion of the centre.

3 Assessment information

3.1 How you will be assessed

Assessment for the unit will stem from a case study scenario which is provided as a background for answers to be provided for all sections. The case study is provided at the end of Section 1.

The responses required are clearly stated at the end of each section. Assessments should incorporate points from the case study into answers but you are free to include other appropriate examples from experience.

This provides the opportunity for candidates to adopt a holistic approach, which is the hallmark of good, modern logistics systems.

3.2 When and where you will be assessed

Assessments are presented in such a way that they are phased to meet the timeframe of delivery of the subject material. The actual time and place of assessment will embrace this approach, the detail being at the discretion of the presenting centre.

International Logistics
Unit Student Guide

China Modern Economic Publishing House

3.3 What you have to achieve

Outcomes 1 and 2 will be assessed in the form of an extended-response question. Achievement will involve covering all points adequately. This involves addressing all of the points in the performance criteria.

It is also possible to assess Outcomes 1–5 by a project based on a case study with extended-response questions.

3.4 Opportunities for reassessment

Normally, you will be given one attempt to pass an assessment with one reassessment opportunity.

Your centre will also have a policy covering 'exceptional' circumstances, for example, if you have been ill for an extended period of time. Each case will be considered on an individual basis and is at your centre's discretion (usually via written application), and they will decide whether or not to allow a third attempt. Please contact your tutor for details regarding how to apply.

Section 1: Systems approach to organisations

4.1 Introduction to this section

What this section is about

This section outlines the systems approach in organisations within the logistics industry, identifying the elements of international logistics systems which are consistent with customer requirements.

Outcomes, aims and objectives

The aim is to provide the skills/knowledge to allow candidates to:

- understand elements of international logistics systems;

- know the inter-relationships between the elements in relation to the strategic objectives of an organisation;

- understand the reasons for the adoption of a systems approach to logistics.

Approximate study time

It is recommended that 12 hours is spent on work for this section with additional time, at discretion of tutor, allowed for assessment work.

Other resources required

Candidates will be expected to carry out some independent research work.

4.2 Assessment information for this section

How you will be assessed

Using the case study scenario provided, Outcomes 1 and 2 will be assessed by an extended-response question. The case study is included at the end of Section 1. The assessment covering Outcomes 1 and 2 is included at the end of Section 2.

When and where you will be assessed

The actual time and place for assessment will be at the discretion of the presenting centre. The extended-response question would normally be completed after completion of the study time for Outcome 2. This is at the discretion of the centre. It may be possible to part complete the assessment at the end of Section 1 and complete it at the end of Section 2.

What you have to achieve

Satisfactory response to extended-response question to cover all performance criteria.

Opportunities for reassessment

Normally, you will be given one attempt to pass an assessment with one reassessment opportunity.

Your centre will also have a policy covering 'exceptional' circumstances, for example if you have been ill for an extended period of time.

Each case will be considered on an individual basis and is at your centre's discretion (usually via written application), and they will decide whether or not to allow a third attempt. Please contact your tutor for details regarding how to apply.

4.3 Elements of an international logistics system

All businesses today work within increasingly internationalised, or globalised, market places. The logistics company operates in the service sector but operators will need knowledge of all sectors in order to compete and keep abreast of changing demands.

A business unit carries out productive activity which results in the creation of goods or services. Business units can be small scale, often sole traders or partnerships, or large scale national or international companies.

To a large extent, the size of the business reflects the amount of capital invested. In the logistics industry there are many one-person businesses. In international logistics there are huge, multinational, companies.

This trend is increasing as products and services are sourced from new markets. It is clear that emerging industrial nations are competing fiercely in the worldwide market place. Competition is viewed as a very positive thing, giving consumers quality products at good prices.

Products sourced at competitive prices must be moved to the markets where the sales take place. The logistics expert provides the means by which this can happen and is required to understand the main aspects of all logistics issues and the ways in which other businesses fit into the system.

All organisations specialise in, or have sectors or divisions who specialise in, some sort of work producing commodities, goods or services. As noted, logistics is a service activity. The main activities undertaken in the logistics industry are discussed later in this section.

The three main types of production are illustrated below.

Basic	Manufacture/process	Tertiary
Production of goods from nature, e.g. oil, coal, gold	Production of products derived from secondary production, e.g. clothes, wine, bricks	Production of services, may be personal or commercial services, e.g. banking, transport, hairdressing
Example of employees	**Example of employees**	**Example of employees**
Oil drillers, fishermen, lumberjacks, coal miners, farmers	Engineers, builders, aeronautical engineers, joiners, decorators	Commercial — retailers, bankers Personal — doctors, policemen, entertainers Logistics operators
Production of goods		**Production of services**

There are a few countries whose economic output still depends mainly on production in the primary production areas (basic production), but all advanced economies have all three types of production in operation at any one given time.

From the table above it is clear that the logistics industry is mainly in the service sector, not producing an actual item such as a television, but being involved in the chain which links the producer with the buyer.

Even operating in primary (basic) production there will be a need to transport goods. In this situation the transport-based aspects of logistics can be easily identified. The need is to get the raw resources and materials to manufacturers and producers who will be hoping to supply goods to meet consumer demand.

The business environment is regularly changing and ever greater demands are being placed by consumers on businesses to:

- meet high-quality standards

- provide products or services quickly and to exact locations

- deliver on time to locations

- provide good design

- offer innovative products

- offer choice

- give good service

- offer convenient service

- offer services more cheaply

- offer services with lower risk.

Within a company or organisation the supply chain consists of different departments, ranging from procurement of materials to customer service. Managing the supply chain well is the aim of most organisations — they want to create a customer-satisfying process, where the effect of the whole supply chain is more important than the effect of each individual department.

They also want to maintain profitability and, increasingly, adopt environmentally friendly policies. The issue of environmental protection will, over the next 10 years, become a major issue for all parts of the logistics industry.

In part, the logistics industry operates at the delivery end of the supply chain, i.e. at the point where customers receive the good or service they want to purchase. That part is the one that most customers will be familiar with. In total, the industry is operating across the supply chain spectrum.

Organisations in a supply chain may sometimes have to forgo increased profits so that business partners make the money they need. The complexities of operating in a supply chain have led organisations to invest heavily in reliable software. Computerised systems help in the logistics industry by helping with:

- forecasting and planning — to successfully direct main operations several categories of software may be required to aid with demand management, i.e. forecasting and planning

- procurement — procurement software helps companies buy at the best prices, for example finding acceptable substitutes, if necessary, and identifying available discounts through volume pricing agreements

- completion — after making plans and placing orders the product must get to the right place at the right time.

4.4 Globalisation

Most advanced economies now operate within worldwide markets. It is no longer possible to close avenues for businesses because of distances between supply and demand for products and services.

It would only take a visit to the local supermarket to show that the range of products for sale has been sourced worldwide.

The logistics industry is at the forefront of what may be viewed as an 'explosion' in demand for transfer of goods worldwide.

This increase in demand brings challenges for the industry with differences in demand depending on where in the operations spectrum an organisation is situated.

Global supply chain management involves a very complicated integration of processes, which is required to manage resources/materials from origins through manufacturing and transport to the consumer.

There are three parts to the work of supply chain managers: they manage the process, operate with partners and monitor the performance of the company. The globalisation of trade will continue to throw up new challenges for supply chain managers.

Below are some quotations about globalisation. They give an indication of the main points to be considered when thinking of the possible effects of globalisation of the marketplace and how logistics managers keep pace with change.

'*(Globalisation is) the intensification of worldwide social relations which link distant localities in such a way that the local happenings are shaped by events occurring many miles away and vice versa.*'

Anthony Giddens, *The Consequences of Modernity,* 1990

'*Our challenge now is to continue to open up. Some people think that globalisation, on which every perceived ill is blamed, has gone too far. They want to turn the clock back to a golden age that never was. I'm old enough to remember those times; the stagnation of the 70's when we lived in glorious isolation. Then, only the rich who could travel overseas had consumer choices. Trying to go back to those old ways is not an option.'*

Mike Moore, Director General,
World Trade Association, 2001

'In recent decades we have watched the free flow of ideas; individuals, investments and industries grow into an organic trend among developed economies. Not only are traditionally traded goods and securities freely exchanged, but so too are crucial assets such as land, companies, software, commercial rights and expertise.

Inevitably, the emergence of the interlinked economy brings with it the erosion of national sovereignty as the power of information directly touches local communities; academic, professional and social institutions and individuals. It is this borderless world that will give participating economies the capacity for boundless prosperity.'

Frank Borgers, *The Myths and Realities of Globalisation*, 1999

'The terminology of globalisation refers unblushingly to

an ideology of the market dictated by the IMF [International Monetary Federation], the World Bank and the G7 [now G8] executive, crowned by Gatt; to a global market in which the United States, having 'won' the cold war, is the moral conductor. It sets the norm not only for free trade but also (in the universalising mode) for human rights, for historical and cultural studies. What is being globalised is, therefore, American style capitalisation and its implicit world view.'

Kenichi Omae, *The Borderless World*, 1990

'You've no choice, this is inevitable… The forces of change driving the future don't stop at national boundaries, don't respect tradition. They wait for no-one and no nation. They are universal.'

Geeta Kapur, *Globalisation and Culture*, 1998

'There is an empty seat at the banquet of globalisation. While international capital trade and businesses feast on open markets, heightened efficiency and vanishing barriers in the new global market place, labour is nowhere to be found. Why has labour been left out?'

Kathleen Newland, *Workers of the World, Now What?*, 1999

'One can only call the political impact of 'globalisation' the pathology of over-diminished expectations. Many over enthusiastic analysts and politicians have gone beyond the evidence in overstating both the extent of the dominance of world markets and ungovernability.'

Paul Hirst & Graham Thompson,
Globalisation in Question, 1996

Activity

 1.1

To familiarise yourself with some of the issues being raised in the logistics industry in relation to the globalisation debate, read the following article produced by the International Transport Federation (ITF) for their conference in 2003.

The article is written from a union perspective but it highlights many of the current issues and concerns expressed by people involved in the logistics industry.

The ITF Congress debates a range of key issues being faced by transport workers around the world. A number of these are put forward by the ITF Executive Board. Below we look at some of the issues which will come onto the floor in Vancouver and which are liable to shape the work programme of the ITF over the next four years.

The rise of logistics in international freight transport

Transnational corporations produce their goods in plants spread around the world and sell them in every market in the world. The globalisation of production and the liberalisation of world trade has placed new demands on transport.

Many of these global corporations have found that the sheer complexity of moving all their components, supplies and finished products around the world at the right time and cost effectively between all their different suppliers, assembly plants, distribution centres and final customers requires them to use specialist logistics companies. Companies are increasingly outsourcing what they call their supply chain or logistics operations.

This demand has created a new generation of freight transportation and logistics companies. Freight transport companies are spreading their operations into shipping, ports, trucking, rail and aviation cargo. The specialist fast-freight companies such as UPS and Federal Express are expanding to become global logistics companies.

Government postal services, which are rapidly being privatised or commercialised, are turning themselves into global transport companies. These companies are intermodal and are developing seamless global transport networks.

In the past, transport networks were built to serve national rather than global transport plans. Transport matters are still usually heavily regulated by national standards and laws. But nowadays, 90 per cent of goods going across national borders are handled by international freight forwarders. It should hardly be a surprise, therefore, that enormous lobbying pressure, increasingly headed by logistics and freight-forwarding companies, is now being deployed to break down such national rules to clear the way for the full liberalisation and globalisation of transport.

The privatisation of ports, airports, airlines and more lately rail companies has not only been about putting public services into private hands. It has also been about relocating transport investment decisions away from those concerned with national economic planning, towards those supporting the global distribution needs of transnational corporations.

Corporations are increasingly developing their plans according to investment and operational strategies which treat transport both as a global industry and an intermodal one. This raises questions for trade unions which at both the national and international level usually organise by specific transport mode. The Congress will look at the need to add cross-sectoral strategies to those of the individual ITF Sections.

Changes in the international trade union movement

The acceleration of globalisation following the end of the Cold War has become the new challenge for the international union movement. The current irrelevance of old ideological divisions has cleared the way for a much more co-ordinated global union response.

The term "Global Unions" has become a kind of brand name representing much stronger co-operation between the major international union bodies. Along with it goes a much more active response to global trends. We have seen the International Confederation of Free Trade Unions (ICFTU) take up a new campaigning role in challenging the role of the World Bank and the World Trade Organisation in pushing liberalisation; developing new tools for influencing the behaviour of global corporations; and defending core labour standards and union rights.

The Global Union Federations (what until very recently we used to call the International Trade Secretariats), like the ITF, which focus on a single major industry or occupation, are working to tackle corporations which employ worldwide workforces and operate to global corporate strategies. The rise of these transnational companies (TNCs) is happening in all industries. New union strategies include negotiating "framework agreements" which set some basic industrial relations standards in TNCs.

The dividing lines between different industries are becoming less clear. The increasing overlap between transport logistics companies and postal services companies is a good example. It means there will need to be a closer working relationship between the ITF and UNI, the global union federation which brings together postal workers' unions. There are lots of similar examples.

The impact of globalisation on every industry, the emergence of privatisation and deregulation as global trends, foreign investment and transnational ownership, all mean that unions fighting to defend jobs and conditions at the local level find that they cannot do this effectively any more without having some influence at a more global level.

This has two important effects. One, it becomes all the more important that the international union bodies are functioning coherently and effectively. Two, there needs to be a much greater awareness of, and involvement in, the activities of these bodies by trade unions. Some of this is to do with structures, but much of it is to do with attitudes and ways of working. Congress will look at how we work within the wider international union movement and at how effective we are in our internationalism.

The popular movement to reform globalisation

It is not just trade unions that are affected by globalisation, but the whole community. It is not just workplaces which are threatened but our whole environment; not just labour rights which have come under attack, but human rights.

Unlike many others affected by globalisation, workers in unions are relatively well organised. Unions have already established forms of dialogue with bodies such as the World Bank to make sure the views of workers are heard (if frequently ignored). But unions are not the only ones who are organised. In many recent mass protests against globalisation in Seattle, Prague, Gothenburg, Genoa and other cities there have been highly organised groups (the large majority of whom do not use the violent methods that have grabbed most of the headlines). The impressive international gathering of the World Social Forum at Porto Alegre in Brazil, which acts as a counterpoint to the World Economic Forum (unions are involved in both), has become a focus for this wide popular movement.

Unions will not agree with all these organisations or everything they say. Some of these groups throw criticisms at, or have very little understanding of, trade unions. Nevertheless, most have concerns about poverty, social justice and basic rights which are at the heart of union concerns. Attempts at dialogue on issues where there had been conflicting views have already led to better understanding.

The emergence of a large, popular movement challenging the values of global markets and global profits is of immense significance to trade unions. But what role, if any, should trade unions seek to play in this movement? Should unions be developing more active alliances with other organisations and, if so, what kind? Should unions keep their concerns focused on employment issues or look at wider social issues too?

Organising workers in informal work

One of the most significant changes in the way that companies organise work in recent years has been the increase in casual forms of employment. Structural change, deregulation and privatisation, together with the increasing use of subcontractors have resulted in thousands of transport jobs in both developed and developing countries being "informalised" by the use of casual and "temporary" work.

While the definitions of what is and what isn't informal work are not always clear, the trends are very clear indeed. The number of secure, well regulated jobs is sharply decreasing. Unprotected jobs are on the rise. The distinction between formal and informal work is becoming increasingly blurred. Work that was previously regulated and protected is becoming more flexible and vulnerable.

In transport, work is often being transferred to people who are legally classed as self-employed. Many road transport companies, for example, now contract owner-operators rather than employ drivers directly. This enables employers to minimise their own liabilities and social costs, while still controlling in every detail the working conditions of the driver. A nominally independent operator may in fact be effectively tied to servicing a single company.

Unions in a number of countries believe that these owner-operators are in a fundamentally different situation from genuinely independent operators who can choose the work they take. Many unions are recruiting these owner-operators into their organisation.

The Congress will be asking a number of central questions. Should unions be organising owner-operators, or other sorts of "informal" workers, or not? Are unions capable of organising these workers? How can the ITF assist unions trying to organise these workers?

Involving women better

Transport is a gender-segregated industry. Although there are some transport unions with more women members than men (notably civil aviation cabin crew), women are often the minority in transport workers' unions.

In preparation for Congress, the ITF has been carrying out a major survey of its unions to determine just how well represented women are, at all levels of trade union activity and structures. How many women general secretaries there are in the ITF, and whether ITF unions need more women activists or more women elected officials, are the kinds of questions the ITF Women's Committee expects the survey will answer.

This is the third time the ITF Women's Conference has been held just prior to Congress. The first, in 1994 in Geneva, agreed that a programme of gender activities should be established. The second was the 1998 New Delhi Conference, after which the first ever ITF Women's Committee was elected.

Both the Women's Conference and Congress in Vancouver will discuss the effects of the globalised transport workplace for women, particularly the challenges posed for women in public urban transport, and for unions recruiting in the growing logistics, distribution and call-centre industries.

Source: www.itfglobal.org

The industry is fairly male dominated but it is interesting to note that the globalisation of the industry results in changing employment patterns. One issue is the change in the gender base of the workforce. The main points to be picked out at this stage are:

1. as globalisation continues apace, the borders between different multinational companies have disappeared, and the focus in many transport jobs is changing from traditional operational functions to

logistics and the transport chain;

2. while women's participation in the logistics workforce is increasing, this is mostly true of part-time and temporary jobs.

What follows is a glance at how women's roles are changing in the industries most affected by globalisation, and how they are bringing new challenges to trade unionism.

Warehousing, dispatch and packaging

In logistics and distribution in Europe the high-tech quality jobs are generally done by men. In office and dispatch work, the workforce is largely female. In warehousing and packaging, the workforce is gender-mixed. At the same time, the discipline of supply chain management dictates that the transport function becomes only a part of an assembly and distribution chain between producer and consumer. This means that women workers who are in this chain, producing and supplying for a particular company, have common interests, which could be served by international trade union links.

Call centre workers

Call centres are hard to define as a sector — they are

more a technology than an industry. However, almost all call centres are in private sector services. Passenger transport, tourism and express parcel delivery companies all use call centres to handle bookings, plan and track journeys. Call centres in themselves have a very strong growth potential and transport is one of the areas (along with communications, financial and business services) tipped for the steepest growth.

Note: The article above provides a good outline of many of the issues in current logistics operations, as do the statements about women in the logistics industry. The article is printed here as part of an activity but should be referred back to throughout this guide. Some small parts of the expected responses to SAQs will assume that the article has been read.

The global economy depends on the ability of modern transportation systems to move materials and components very rapidly around the world. The transportation systems are well-structured, sophisticated logistics and distribution chains. Multinational companies require speedy delivery of completed goods to distributors and customers.

As discussed at many points in this unit, this activity rarely involves a single-firm operation. It is increasingly operated in a system of sub-contraction and partnership arrangements.

Lean production (sometimes referred to as just in time production) means that the supply of materials and components is organised on demand. This makes companies vulnerable to disruptions in the supply chain as production will come to a halt if goods are not delivered on time. This issue has implications for stock control, warehousing, etc. (discussed in Section 3).

Self-Assessed Question

 1.1

What are the implications for international logistics of the globalisation of the marketplace?

4.5 Logistics ... what is it?

It is sometimes the case that people think of the logistics industry as the transport industry. They will not be aware of the true complexity of the logistics industry. It is, therefore, a good thing to make sure that a true picture of the breadth of operation within the industry is identified.

Asking the question 'What is logistics?' will help to give a clear indication of the areas of work covered within the industry.

In answer to the question:

Logistics may be seen as a process which operates within a company, interacting with many departments and interfacing with:

- external companies

- sellers

- customers

- transport operators.

Logistics is involved at each stage of the movement of goods from the seller to the delivery to customers. The moves can include warehousing and distribution. It involves much more than shipping, receiving, warehousing or transporting.

Logistics is a process moving from the seller's workplace to the customer's door.

The logistics industry will be involved in several activities and issues. The activities include movement of products and information. The issues include costs, integration, timing, service and competitiveness. There will be a number of organisations involved, including carriers, bankers, information companies, communications companies and traders.

Some of the main considerations relating to the issues within the logistic industry in the current global markets are described below.

Product movement

This is often the way logistics is perceived. However, product movement is part of the corporate strategy of an organisation. Where emphasis is on good customer care, cost minimisation, work study, etc., product should be moved in a manner which is consistent with, and complements, the overall company strategy. To maintain a supply chain, products should flow between and among sellers, manufacturing sites, customers and warehouses.

If there is not a genuine flow of products there will be imbalances in inventories and parts and finished goods not being in the correct location.

Geographically, raw materials and products move

between and within all regions of the world. Other departments in a company might concentrate on a narrow geographical base for sourcing, sales or manufacturing. In logistics everything must move — they concentrate on all three, i.e. sourcing, sales and manufacture, and deal in worldwide terms.

It is also necessary to incorporate flexibility in all planning. Forecasting can sometimes be an inexact science.

So many things can happen to change situations. Logistics managers must be able to deal with emergencies, changes in circumstances and business swings.

Many logistics companies have multi-level service programmes in order to keep the global supply chain flowing smoothly.

Information movement

The main aim is to move products and materials. However, up-to-date, accurate information is absolutely essential if good decisions are to be made. It is necessary to know where the products and materials are at any given time. It is also necessary to know what the inventories are and when it may be necessary to take action if anything goes wrong.

It is necessary to know when orders are coming in and when/where they are to be delivered. For this complex operation information must be accurately transferred between companies, carriers, suppliers, warehouses and customers.

There must also be information flow between internal departments such as sales, marketing, purchasing, accounting, internal and external customers. There must be systems in place to deal with all these complex issues.

Service issues

It is essential to respond to the needs in the market, i.e. forecast changes, customer needs, product innovation, sourcing issues. All changes must be managed quickly. Any company that cannot respond will lose customers to those who can. The more diverse the geographical marketplace for sellers, manufacturers, warehouses and customers, the more important time is because distance means time but delays are not acceptable.

Costs

Logistics effectiveness is mainly measured by costs. These involve freight costs, labour costs, warehouse costs and delivery costs. Higher costs do not always guarantee a better service but cost does have a relation to service. Costs and service implications form the basis of operating costs and budgets.

Issues such as currency fluctuations and conversions must be taken into account.

Integration

It is essential that everyone in the company works to satisfy customer needs. The issues relating to customer satisfaction are explored further in other parts of this guide.

Figure 1.1 illustrates most of the main activities in the logistics industry.

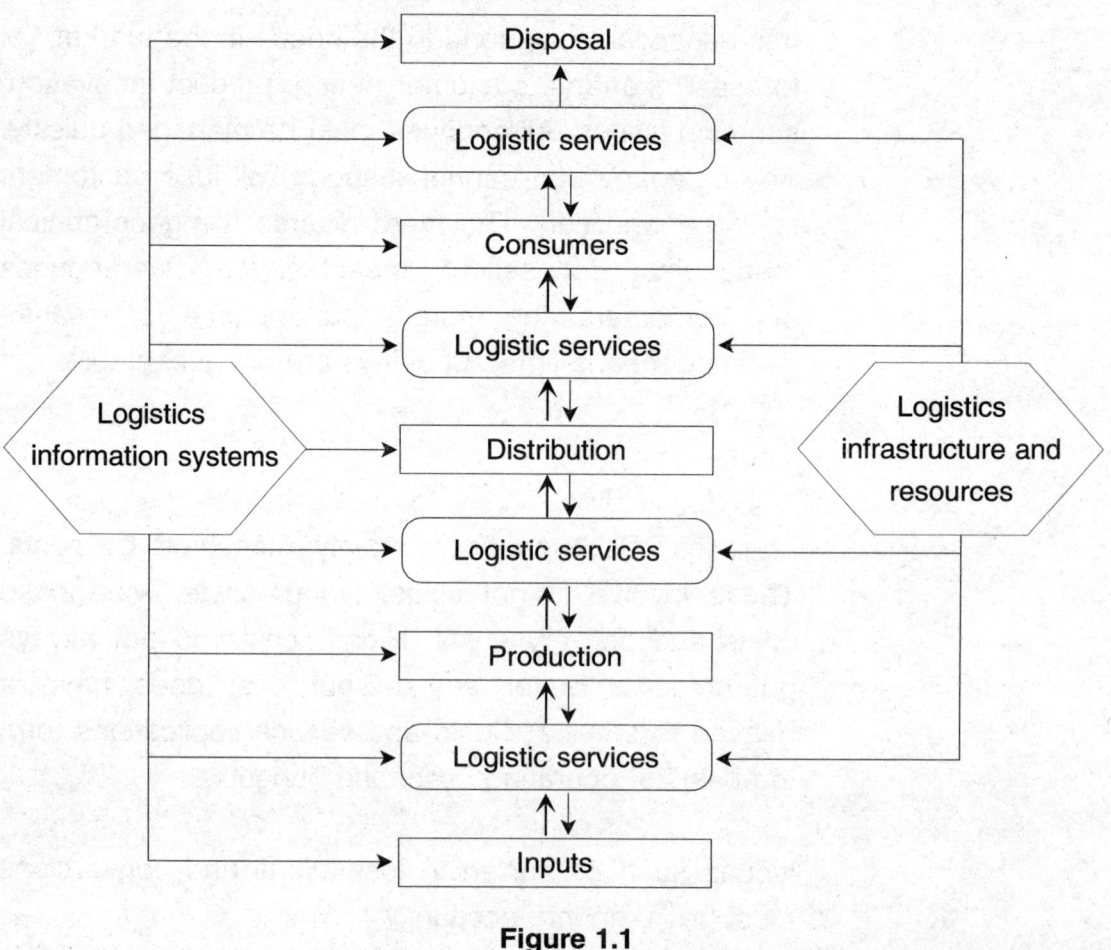

Figure 1.1

Activity

 1.2

Think of some jobs created by the transport and logistics industry, and list them.

Self-Assessed Question

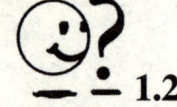 1.2

1. What do we mean by the term 'logistics'?

2. Which main means of transport is used within the logistics industry?

3. If a person is driving a lorry they will be working in front line transport operation. Is this part of logistics?

4. Explain why most people involved in the back-up to lorry transportation also work in logistics.

4.6 Strategic and operational planning

Strategic planning

Strategic planning can be used to determine mission, vision, values, goals, objectives and responsibilities. Every organisation needs to have a strategy otherwise decisions will be made in a vacuum. Companies cannot simply react to events. They must be proactive by planning for the future and keeping up with what their main competitors are doing.

Strategic management is a management tool and is used for the following main purposes:

- to help the organisation do a better job

- to focus the organisation's energy

- to ensure that members of the organisation are working towards the same goals

- to assess and adjust the organisation's direction in response to a changing environment

- to provide a disciplined effort to produce fundamental decisions and actions that shape and guide what an organisation is, what it does and why it does it whilst focusing on the future

- to continue a process of planning because it involves

intentionally setting goals, i.e. choosing a desired future and developing an approach to achieving these goals

- to allow for built-in assumptions that an organisation must be responsive to a dynamic, changing environment

- to make sure that decisions are made that will ensure the organisation's ability to successfully respond to changes in the environment, keep pace with competitors and satisfy customers' needs.

Strategic planning is often referred to as long-term planning but this is confusing. They may be taking place at the same time but long-term planning focuses more on the development of a plan for accomplishing a goal over a period of time.

Strategic planning assumes that the organisation must be responsive to a changing world. This planning stresses the need to make decisions that will allow the business to successfully respond to possible future changes.

In essence planning must be translated into good strategic management decisions where there is a definite purpose in mind, a good understanding of the environment and a development of effective responses.

Operational planning

Operational plans should establish the activities for each part of the organisation for a future time period. They link the strategic plan with the activities the company will deliver and the resources needed to deliver them.

Operational plans should be prepared by the people who will be involved in implementation. There is often a need for significant cross-departmental dialogue as plans created by one part of the organisation inevitably have implications for other parts.

Operational plans should contain:

- clear objectives

- activities to be delivered

- quality standards

- desired outcomes

- staffing and resource requirements

- implementation timetables

- a process for monitoring progress.

This helps to set out clearly the implementation of the strategic plan against specific objectives. Like the strategic plan, the operational plan should be simple and easily understood by all participants.

All staff should know what they have to do and the timescales within which they must do it.

A good operational plan can be used to review and learn from both mistakes and good practice:

- What went well?

- What went badly?

- Why?

- What were the costs and where could savings be made?

- What processes could be simplified?

Learning from these issues can save a lot of time and money when planning the next operational period.

Strategic and operational planning are the most used strategies. There are other levels, as illustrated in the table below adapted from the work of Lucey.

Level 1 Current operations	Level 2 Operational planning	Level 3 Tactical planning	Level 4 Strategic planning
What operations need to be carried out by existing personnel with facilities to meet specific outputs in the coming operational period? What is the quality of our management?	What finance, materials, plant and equipment are needed for the immediate future? Manning levels? Incentives? What are the best methods of organising these to meet operational requirements?	What changes are due from our strategic plans? What new plant, equipment, information systems and working methods are needed to implement the new plans?	What business(es)? How should we organise/structure/ finance the new plans and allocate resources?
Time: the present	Time: 1–12 months	Time: 1–5 years	Time: 3–5 years

Problems with planning

Many managers do not view planning as a key part of their job because, for example, planning is time-consuming — managers will often claim that they do not have enough time at the present:

- there are more urgent tasks to be done

- planning requires a clear head

- taking action feels better than thinking about it

- having a plan reduces freedom of action and restrains creativity

- nobody takes any notice of plans once they are written

- having a plan may tie into targets that are difficult to meet

- there is not enough information to plan properly.

We now recognise these as excuses or call them good reasons, but planning is the key to the efficient and effective running of an organisation.

Self-Assessed Question

 1.3

Strategic planning requires attention to the 'big picture' and willingness to adapt to changing circumstances. Explain.

Human resource planning

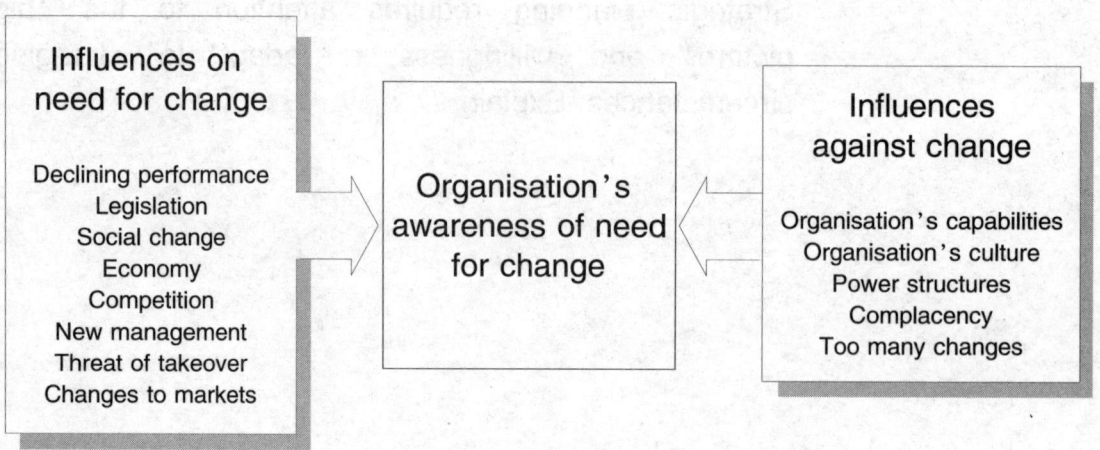

Worldwide information technology enables global markets to operate. It has created entire new industries and improved efficiencies.

Organisations need to worry about their own systems and operations as well as those of their suppliers and customers. Any company operating in worldwide logistics needs to have good planning strategies.

One of the most important planning issues is that of having the best, trained and competent staff. This issue is often lost among the other pressing issues which focus on meeting costs, deadlines, etc. Without good staff none of these targets are possible.

Globalisation has made it possible to outsource manufacturing or service support to a variety of locations.

Some human resource issues have far-reaching implications for companies. Currently many UK call centre jobs have been outsourced to India, where labour is cheaper, as company chief executives are required to minimise total costs. A worldwide logistics operation will require staff in each of its customer networks.

Planning is never easy:

In developing strategies for planning it may be appropriate to consider Deming's 14-point management philosophy:

1. Create constancy of purpose for continual improvement of products and services.

2. Adopt commitment to seek continual improvements.

3. Switch from detecting defects to preventing them, i.e. from inspection at the end of the process to getting it right first time, every time.

4. When dealing with suppliers focus on quality of product, reliability of delivery, co-operation and

improvement. *Note:* Not price.

5. Improvement is not confined to products and processes but extends to *all* supporting services and activities.

6. Train using modern techniques.

7. Supervision should not be 'chasing' but coaching and supporting.

8. Drive out fear and encourage two-way communication.

9. Remove barriers between departments.

10. Do not have unrealistic targets.

11. Eliminate quotas and numeric targets.

12. Remove barriers that prevent employees having pride in the work that they perform.

13. Encourage education and self-improvement for everyone.

14. Publish top management's permanent commitment to continuous improvement of quality and productivity.

Not all of the points in the management philosophy will be important for all companies. If they are used (all or in part) successfully they will help in promoting a culture of customer care and create/maintain an environment for that culture to continue.

Good systems stretching across the entire organisation will provide lasting benefits.

In as complex an industry as logistics, a systems approach is probably essential. As the level of precision and efficiency demanded of the industry (and of technology science and management in general) increases it is necessary to concentrate on organisational goals, managing within complex systems and considering the following four concepts in the approach.

1. **Specialisation:** A system is divided into smaller components, allowing more specialised concentration on each component.

2. **Grouping:** To avoid generating greater complexity with increasing specialisation, it becomes necessary to group related disciplines or sub-disciplines.

3. **Coordination :** As the components and subcomponents of a system are grouped, it is necessary to coordinate the interactions among groups.

4. **Emergent properties:** Dividing a system into subsystems (groups of component parts within the

system), requires recognising and understanding the 'emergent properties' of a system; that is, recognising why the system as a whole is greater than the sum of its parts. For example, two forest stands may contain the same tree species, but the spatial arrangement and size structure of the individual trees will create different habitats for wildlife species. In this case, an emergent property of each stand is the wildlife habitat.

4.7 Economic factors

The many practitioners within the logistics industry face their own special challenges, but all operate within an economic system and are, therefore, influenced by economic factors.

Whatever is produced it is not possible to satisfy wants — these develop and extend with every advance in technology, e.g. advanced technology allows many activities to produce even smaller and more sophisticated mobile phones.

In everyday language, the word 'cost' means the amount of money that has to be given up in order to obtain a particular good or service. In economic language the term 'opportunity cost' expresses the cost of a commodity not in money but in terms of the alternative foregone.

If we exercise choice we must have alternatives from which to choose; consumers and organisations alike make choices.

All economic activity occurs within a political framework. The entrepreneur will have the ideas, combine the resources and take the risks with the aim of making a profit. If there were no other factors to consider the entrepreneur would set a price for the goods/services and the consumer would purchase if they could afford the price.

In economic systems, nothing is as simple as that, but the main economic goal of profitability remains. Some purchases are in cash, but increasingly goods and services are bought on credit, i.e. borrowing money to varying extents. Consumers operate in world markets — cash flows, inflation, exchange rates and interest rates being of vital importance. Operators at all points of the supply chain must be aware of the following economic factors in order to survive.

Interest rates

In understanding interest rates and how they affect the business, it is necessary to know that the key to using interest rates to aid economic management is the effect that they have on demand. If inflationary pressure is rising, an increase in the rate of interest will dampen down the growth of aggregate demand. Demand falls when interest rates rise.

Aggregate demand is:

consumption + investment + government expenditure + (exports − imports)

Interest rate changes are very important for the businesses in the following situations:

1. Consumption

Consumption will fall when interest rates are raised. This happens for two reasons. The first reason is that it is now more expensive to borrow money. People will be reluctant to borrow, so lower borrowing results in lower spending. It is not just borrowing money that is affected, but also people who are still paying off existing borrowing, e.g. mortgage holders. There is a reduction in disposable income, i.e. the amount of cash remaining after all bills have been paid, and therefore less money to spend. The same will be true for people who do not pay off their full credit card balances each month.

2. Investment

To invest, many firms will, like individuals, have to borrow. They will borrow if they think that the rate of return on their investment is greater than the interest rate. If interest rates rise fewer investment projects are likely to be viable as the higher cost of borrowing money will mean the projects become less profitable.

Interest rate rises therefore reduce the level of investment.

Sterling exchange rate

The interest rate influences the exchange rate because it influences the supply and demand of currencies on the foreign exchange markets.

Businesses must be aware that a good deal of trade in foreign currencies is for speculative purposes as traders will move funds from one currency to another in order to take advantage of price movements or to take advantage of better returns in different countries.

For example, if the interest rate in the USA was 3% but was 5% in the UK, there may be advantages gained from transferring funds in dollar-based securities to those based in sterling. This can be understood by thinking of moving funds from a bank that only pays 3% interest on savings accounts to another bank that pays 5% interest on savings accounts.

What is likely to happen is:

A rise in the interest rate will lead to a rise in the values of sterling against other currencies. This is called appreciation.

Other things being equal, an appreciation of the

exchange rate will lead to:

- a rise in export prices in the UK

- a fall in import prices in the UK.

This is turn would be expected to have an effect on the demand for both imports and exports, which would result in:

- demand for exports would fall as export prices rise

- demand for imports would rise as import prices fall.

Inflation

When there is a rise in general prices, interest rates rise because the lenders of money know that they are going to be repaid in money whose purchasing power will have fallen since the time between granting the loan and receiving the repayment.

The higher interest rate is to compensate for the loss of purchasing power. Borrowers of money may hesitate to go ahead with a purchase of interest-sensitive goods, such as cars, computers, etc. A rise in general prices decreases real wealth for all those who hold their assets in money form.

Synergy and trade-off

One of the basic operational difficulties involved in the supply chain responsiveness/cost-efficient balance is that the relationship between supply chain cost and responsiveness is characterised by trade-off.

Once a set of objectives have been set it will most often be the case that priorities will have to be identified. This prioritisation is required because of time and budget constraints, and in some instances security issues.

The systematic approach to this situation will be slightly different for organisations at different parts of the supply chain and within different branches of the logistics industry. The constant approach to maintaining responsiveness may be understood from the following illustration:

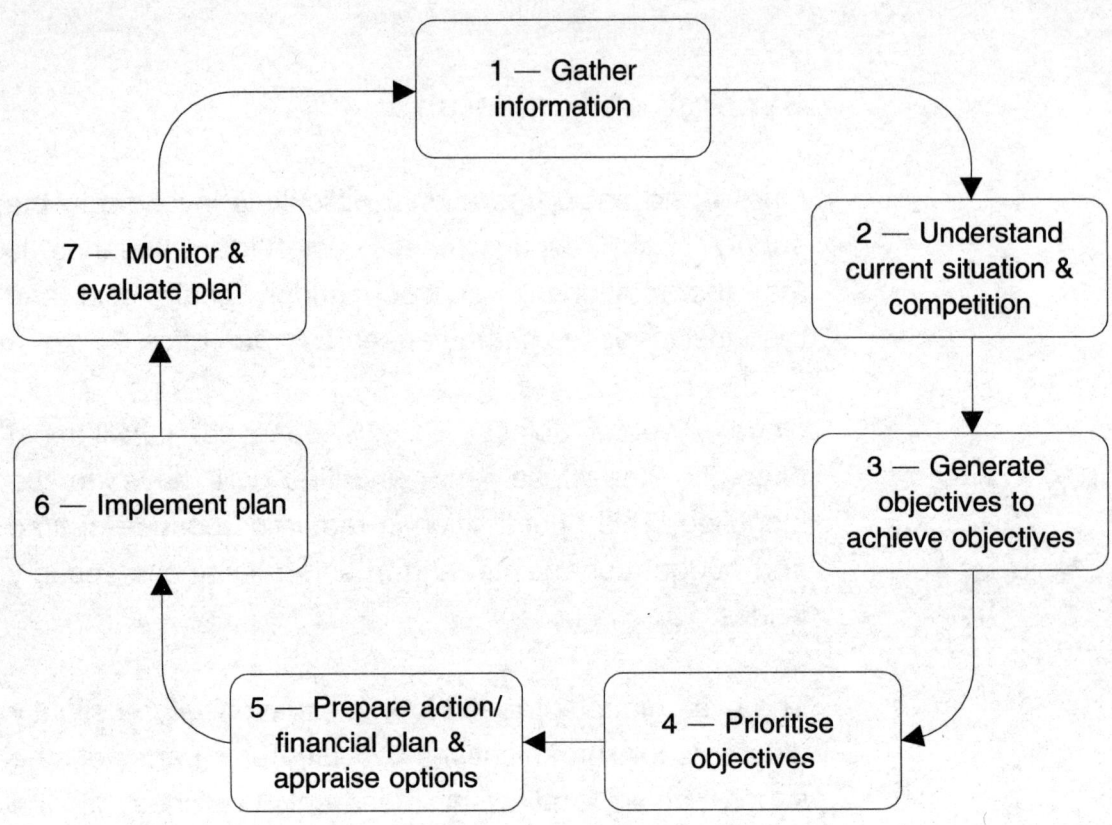

The synergistic relationship is made clear by showing the many facets of supply chain responsiveness. Four points worth noting are:

1. By focusing on identification and use of synergy, supply chain managers are in a better position to identify and take actions that, at the same time, put responsiveness up while driving costs down.

2. Strict adherence to inventory control can have

adverse effects on supply chain responsiveness (inventory control is discussed in Section 3).

3. By focusing on specific dimensions of responsiveness managers increase the potential to identify synergistic relationships that can be exploited for competitive advantage.

4. Depending on the market segment in which a company competes, it cannot position itself on responsiveness as a whole but on specific dimensions of it.

In logistics, as in any other organisation, good performance is achieved through efficient structures and ongoing capital investment. A broad range of measures will be used to monitor key indicators such as efficiency, profitability, corporate growth, market share and costs.

Performance must be supported by a system of measurement.

Measurement is particularly significant in the current international logistics situation as rapid growth has been a critical factor over the past 20 years and there is no sign of a slowdown in this trend.

Every indication shows that there will be growth in Internet shopping and this will in turn generate more demand for 'door to door' services.

Finally, for every part of the logistics process to operate efficiently it is necessary to do several things:

1. Clearly define the elements of international logistics systems.

2. Identify the relationships of all at each part of the supply chain.

3. Understand the need for strategic, operational and human resource planning.

4. Identify the main economic pressures.

5. Identify the main points in terms of synergy and trade-off.

6. Realise that a systems approach is necessary to enhance performance.

Given the changes in the business marketplace that affect logistics operations, such as emerging technologies and industry initiatives, developing and using a formal logistics strategy to guide your operations is now more important than ever.

The case for creating a logistics strategy

The process of developing a logistics strategy does

more than just create the strategy itself. The discovery processes involved can:

- enhance intra-company communications.

- identify potential areas of weakness.

- identify untapped sources of competitive advantage such as cooperative supply chain initiatives that could be the key to maintaining future cost competitiveness and solid client relationships.

Despite these inherent benefits, surveys report that only 40% of senior logistics professionals have a formal logistics strategy in place.

Faced with regional consolidations, resource and cost reduction plans, operating and customer issues and industry initiatives, the logistics professionals have no time left for the critical tasks. Furthermore, some may not have got the required training in the logistics strategy's process, components and methods.

Nevertheless, new technologies and changing distribution channels make it critical for every firm to foresee the impact of these coming changes and position their operations proactively. Developing a logistics strategy can be critical.

Overcoming the barriers to create a logistics strategy

To create a powerful logistics strategy, you need data. Fortunately, today the information required for both tactical and strategic logistics operations planning is easier to obtain than ever before. Advances in both operating systems and computing power make it much easier and economical to effectively perform these tasks.

You will also need a solid understanding of basic logistics, industry business dynamics, current and emerging technologies and initiatives, and most importantly, an understanding of your firm's current and future goals within the marketplace. Like any complex task, developing a logistics strategy is a skill that is acquired, refined and improved each time you use it.

What developing a logistic strategy entails

Briefly, you need to analyse all components of supply chain and operations, looking for the potential for cost benefits and competitive advantage, including customer service requirements. The component areas of a complete logistics strategy should include:

- vision development
- transportation
- outsourcing
- logistics systems
- competitors
- human resources
- network design
- supply chain
- information
- options analysis
- strategy review
- communications.

4.8 Summary of this section

The overarching purpose of this section is to explain the systems approach to organisation in the context of the logistics activity. In doing this the elements of international logistics systems have been outlined alongside the interrelationships between the elements in relation to the strategic objectives of the organisations.

There has been a clear argument set out for the adoption of a systems approach to logistics, related to organisational performance.

4.9 Answers to SAQs

SAQ 1.1

Change is never easy, but organisations in a global marketplace must be willing to embrace change when necessary. For commercial organisations threats are not only posed by local firms, but also by companies worldwide.

Traditional political and physical barriers between countries have been replaced by international trading regions such as the European Union. Transport and communication costs have reduced, in relative terms, thus increasing the potential for global competitors to enter what were once domestic markets.

Markets have become more open and consumers the world over have generally become more sophisticated. Organisations who do not embrace change will probably be pushed out of the market in a globalised system.

SAQ 1.2

Logistics is involved in each stage of the movement of goods: from the seller to the delivery to customers. Logistics services can be considered in terms of four major groups of activities:

1. production processes (production flow management, inventory management, packaging, order processing, demand forecasting)

   o materials and other inputs (procurement, materials management)

   o transport and storage

   o product support (parts and services)

   o reverse flows and disposal (product/equipment returns, recycling, waste)

The infrastructure and resources used to provide logistics services comprise:

   o human resources (managerial and operational)

   o financial resources

   o packaging materials

- warehousing (land, buildings, plant and equipment)
- transport (e.g. pallets, containers, vehicles, terminals)
- communications facilities, equipment and software.

2. Railways, roads, sea, air internal waterways.

3. If someone arranges for a lorry to collect and deliver goods and looks after them in a warehouse, that person works in the logistics industry.

Similarly, someone dealing with the planning and documentation for the transport of goods and people (before and after completion) works in the industry.

4. The main point is included in 3 above.

SAQ 1.3

Strategic planning is used to determine mission, vision, values, goals, objectives and responsibilities. Every organisation needs to have a strategy otherwise decisions will be made in a vacuum.

If no-one knows how to approach the main aims and objectives it will be impossible to offer a comprehensive service. It is a management tool and is used for helping the organisation do a better job, ensuring everyone has the same goals, assess and adjust, shape and guide the organisation.

4.10 Answers to activities

Activity 1.1

This is a reading activity therefore there is no one answer given. The activity may form the background to group discussion and can be referred back to throughout the study of this pack.

Activity 1.2

- Rail signalman
- Bus driver
- LGV driver
- Airline pilot
- Port operator
- Taxi driver
- Courier
- Freight forwarder
- Distribution manager
- Warehouse manager
- Logistics manager
- Merchant navy officer.

4.11 Case study

The case study can be used the base for consideration of answers to the SAQs.

Case study scenario

Craigens Transportation started as a one-man haulage company 25 years ago. At that time most of the journeys were made within a 50-mile radius of head office, gradually expanding to provide a UK-wide service. For many years this remained the situation. In the past 10 years the founder's two sons have joined the business and the expansion in that time has been immense. The company now deals with suppliers from all parts of the world and offers transportation, warehousing, returns management and recycling advice.

Throughout the past 10 years the company have provided practical logistics solutions on both strategic and operational issues within the supply chain. Assignments range from large strategic projects lasting for months to smaller activities such as reviewing a company's transport plans. Some clients are large multinational companies, some are very small one-person businesses.

Customer service is at the heart of the company's philosophy. The need for repeat orders alongside a desire to reduce returns and keep the customer perceiving that the company has offered the very best service drive this approach.

A team of consultants employed to review ways of becoming more efficient and provide enhanced customer service advised the introduction of a reliable electronic data system. The system was to be outsourced to a company (Edisol) offering appropriate expertise and the ability to deliver solutions on time and in budget.

A dedicated Electronic Data Interchange (EDI) manager was employed within the company and the new system was set up. The system proved to be reliable, fully supported by Edisol and compatible with current systems. Administration overheads were considerably reduced. This was achieved, in part, because of a huge reduction in recalls and returns.

5 Section 2: The importance of customer service

5.1 Introduction to this section

What this section is about

The section is concerned with the importance of customer service to the provision of a competitive logistics and distribution strategy.

Outcomes, aims and objectives

Candidates will be expected to:

- identify the elements of customer service appropriate to the business;

- evaluate the contribution of customer service to buyer/supplier relationships;

- explain the customer service approach to logistics and distribution.

Approximate study time

12 hours.

Other resources required

There are no other resources required. However, as suggested in the introductory section of the guide it is expected throughout that access to newspapers, Internet, etc. is used.

5.2 Assessment information for this section

How you will be assessed

Outcomes 1 and 2 are assessed by an extended-response question covering all the performance criteria for both outcomes. The case study scenario on which all assessment is based is printed at the end of Section 1. The questions are printed at the end of this section.

When and where you will be assessed

Assessment will take place at an appropriate point of study and at a place decided by tutors and centre staff.

What you have to achieve

Satisfactory completion of extended-response question.

Opportunities for reassessment

Normally, you will be given one attempt to pass an assessment with one reassessment opportunity.

Your centre will also have a policy covering 'exceptional' circumstances, for example if you have been ill for an extended period of time. Each case will be considered on an individual basis and is at your centre's discretion (usually via written application), and they will decide whether or not to allow a third attempt. Please contact your tutor for details regarding how to apply.

5.3 Elements of customer service

Always the first question to be asked is 'Who are the customers'? This will be answered relative to the business or industry in which the questioner is operating.

An initial simple definition might be:

'People who want and can afford to buy goods or services.'

This may be too simple. The Institute of Customer Services suggests there are two kinds of customers: internal and external.

External customers are those who have no connection to the organisation and to a large extent fit the above definition.

This might include shoppers, passengers, patients, clients or students. Increasingly customers may be located in all parts of the world far from the original point of production or despatch of goods/services.

It may include you as you are undertaking a course of study. Customers will often be asked to fill out customer survey reports. This will be of increasing importance because of the physical distance between suppliers and purchasers. The way questions are phrased in very important but some of them may be:

- Did this work for you?

- Was the material suitable?

- Was it clear to you what you had to do?

- Was the material relevant?

All organisations are almost certainly customers of other organisations. Sometimes it is easy to imagine that the customer is an individual and the supplier a business organisation, but brief reflection for a minute makes us realise that this is certainly not the case.

The following list gives examples of goods demanded by individuals and companies:

- wines and beers

- food

- vehicles

- mobile telephones

- computers

- electrical goods

- clothing.

You will certainly be aware that in all these areas the

market is worldwide. You will also possibly shop in a large super- or hypermarket in which there is a full range of goods and, increasingly, services available to you. The latter could include insurance, personal loans, holidays, etc.

In the past 10 years large supermarket chains have enlarged their product and services range considerably. Consumers may now take it for granted that they can shop for clothes and food in the same shop or with the same company via the Internet.

In order to be able to obtain the range of goods and services which we demand these organisations have become the external customers of other organisations.

People now want the food they like to be available all the year round. The production of food is, to a large extent, seasonal, so suppliers will range around the world and obtain what is wanted from wherever it is currently available.

The produce must be transported to the appropriate market locations. This is the work we can identify within international logistics.

Internal customers include those working in different parts of the business. An organisation may have many departments or sections.

One department may have 'inputs' from another

department, modify or 'add value' to these inputs then 'output' them to other departments.

In this sense then departments are acting as customers for one another. Some global organisations have sections in many countries worldwide.

Each section may have a particular specialism and will, therefore, be part of the supply chain for another section of the company.

Activity

 2.1

Based on an organisation you know (from either an internal or external viewpoint) make short lists of both internal and external customers. (If you cannot think of a company that you know about consider a large organisation such as Marks & Spencer.)

Meeting your customer needs

When it is clear what is meant by internal and external customers it is possible to identify who the customers are. It is then possible to address the needs of those customers.

Generally customers want the same things:

- the right product/service

- at the right price

- at the right time

- in the right place

- positive and helpful service

- to be listened to

- to be understood

- to be cared for

- to be treated intelligently

- to be treated as an individual.

If asked what they want, in terms of service, a

customer would probably say, I want you to:

- make it easy for me

- be efficient, dependable, trustworthy and accurate

- only tell me about things which are relevant to my needs

- know about me

- inspire me with confidence in your organisation

- surprise me with your service

- willingly help me

- be reliable and keep your promises

- treat me as an individual

- make it easy for me to trust you

- show me that you have the technical and organisational knowledge to help me

- do things differently sometimes.

It seems that the most commonly used word by customers is 'right'. This is a byword for quality. The goods must arrive at the correct location, on time and as requested.

Total quality management (TQM) is the approach which states that all people in an organisation have individual as well as collective responsibility for maintaining high quality standards.

The idea is:

Get it right, first time and every time.

W.E. Deming is regarded by the Japanese as the person who introduced TQM into Japan after the Second World War.

If you improve quality:

- you reduce costs

- you improve productivity.

This allows you to:

- reduce prices

- increase your market share

- stay in business.

It is always essential to obtain accurate information about customer needs. If that is constantly done the marketing information used will ensure that customer needs are met wherever possible. Sometimes it is necessary to do some market research to make absolutely certain of being 'in tune' with customers (it is possible to think that customer needs are being met but sometimes, instead of giving feedback, customers simply change to other suppliers.

Consider Figure 2.1. It illustrates the ongoing process of market research necessary to be constantly aware of customer needs:

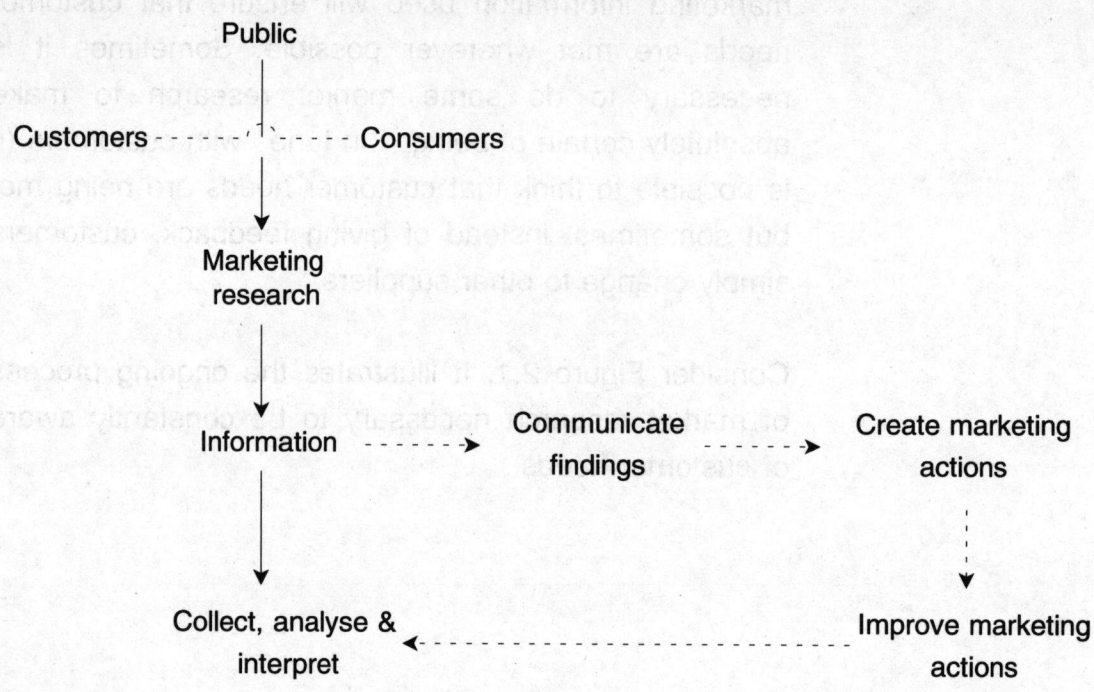

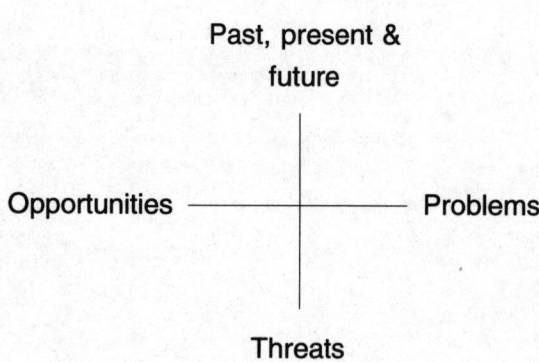

Figure 2.1
Source: Essentials of Market Research, **Tony Proctor**

Self-Assessed Question

 2.1

You have been asked by your immediate manager to meet an external customer who is important to your firm regarding a possible further order for your firm's services. You know that the person who is coming is very thorough and precise. You know you will be closely questioned on all aspects of the service. The meeting is due to take place in 3 days' time. What are the skills you will need to meet this customer's needs (and possibly exceed them)?

Maintaining customer loyalty and satisfaction

It is most likely that organisations consider customer loyalty by referring to a customer whom an organisation has managed to retain over a period of time continually returning to purchase the organisation's goods or services. This is generally referred to as customer retention.

Activity

 2.2

Consider the following:

- advocates (recommend product)

- regular customers

- occasional users

- one-off purchasers.

Which of the above would you wish to have if you were part of an organisation?

Customer satisfaction

In order to provide satisfaction for customers it is necessary for organisations to understand the full requirements and needs, expectations and attitudes of the customer, which reflect his/her perception of satisfaction.

Internal customers will have opportunities to express concerns directly so it is on external customers that most activity is concentrated.

Most organisations maintain customer records. They will often use this information as the basis for establishing, as they see it, customer loyalty.

They might look at the length of time a person has been a customer or how many times a customer has purchased products. In other words, the techniques might not really involve the customer at all. But for customer satisfaction it is the customer's perception that is important.

Organisations must therefore use techniques that allow them to interpret customer responses. These could include interviews, seeking complaints, surveys, questionnaires and telephone calls.

An elementary comparison of customer needs now and

those of 20 years ago would probably show that current customers:

- demand more access/time

- are less willing to wait

- demand faster responses

- want more information

- have less patience with broken service promises

- complain more, and are increasingly assertive.

These are not easy factors to satisfy. The points (above) may apply equally to internal and external customers. Indeed, they are very important to internal customers.

This can be neatly summed up in Figure 2.2, found in a number of sources and identifying four key areas.

A working definition of customer satisfaction might be:

'The establishment of a positive and ongoing relationship between organisations and customers who purchase the organisation's goods and services and which establish, in customers, the belief that their needs are being fully met.'

This is not a constant and it is necessary to monitor service constantly in order to maintain satisfaction. All parts of the definition are important.

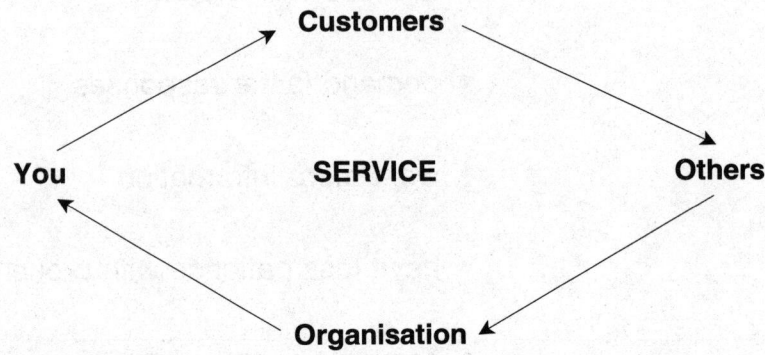

Figure 2.2　The four key areas of customer service.

Self-Assessed Question

 2.2

State clearly what is meant by the term 'customer satisfaction'.

Self-Assessed Question

 2.3

What questions might you ask in an organisation that hopes to apply total quality management?

Self-Assessed Question

2.4

Why would a company adopt a total quality management approach to customer care?

External customer satisfaction

As mentioned, it might be easier to find out if internal customers are satisfied and it may equally be possible to get mixed messages for external customers. If a product is sold to a customer who seems very pleased with what has been provided but does not re-order, would that be taken as an indication of customer satisfaction?

In his book *Excellence*, Tom Peters quotes a chief executive officer who spent a great deal of his time asking customers:

'*How are we doing for you?*'

He taught his staff the philosophy:

'*Complaints are golden!* '

He meant that if you are not getting customer feedback you do not really know how you are performing in the market and could well be losing market share without being aware of it.

On the basis of customer complaints he would involve staff and change strategy, process, materials and methods to achieve customer satisfaction. Changing strategy is, of course, quite drastic yet this senior executive would undo anything he thought was not working and change direction in a major way if that was thought necessary. But remember that he involved staff — the 'internal customers'!

Peters also points out that:

'Satisfaction belongs to the customers.'

'It is their perception of it which matters. Their perception is reality!'

The ongoing problem, of course, is that customers are human beings, in all their bewildering variety, particularly in attitudes towards goods and services.

Each year a survey (the JD Power Customer Service Index) is carried out in the UK. This ranks cars against a range of factors identified by those who purchase cars as being the major reasons for their choices. On the basis of perception, it would be realistic to expect cars made in Germany to feature strongly.

German cars in the UK are widely seen to be well built and engineered. Yet in the top 10 cars in the survey, six are Japanese, two are from the expensive end of the German product list, one is Swedish and the other is German inspired but built in Czechoslovakia! Most of the popular German cars in each of the categories covered perform little better than average. This might illustrate Peters' point that perception is all.

How did the perception about cars come about? Most likely it was because relationships with customers were built upon meeting their needs, then checking up on their needs — listening to them and actively seeking out their views — then, and here is where loyalty is established, acting upon their views.

To build relationships with customers the Institute of Customer Services advises that it is necessary to:

- build confidence in the level of service provided

- meet the ongoing needs and expectations of your customers

- continue to develop the relationship between your customers and your organisation.

Great stress is laid on developing relationships between internal customers, including suppliers. It is of little benefit to establish the views of external customers but be unable to implement what needs to be done within the organisation.

It should be clear to you by now that you must be able to identify who your customers are within and outside your organisation. You must be able to establish their needs and their expectations and once you have done so, set in motion the activities to meet, and indeed exceed, their needs and expectations.

Customer dissatisfaction

We have already mentioned that it may be easier to identify internal customer satisfaction. Some of the indications of dissatisfaction might be poor productivity, poor quality output, perhaps arguments between departments and low morale, indicated by high sickness and absenteeism rates.

Customer service

This is a subsection of customer care. Customer care is the overall set of attitudes and culture in a firm or company, which determines how it deals with all its customers. Customer service is the set of skills that those who are employed by a company or firm possess. They will include:

- awareness

- behaviour

- technical skills

- teamwork.

Activity

 2.3

Make a short list of large organisations which you believe have established themselves as those which provide both customer satisfaction and loyalty.

Then make a short list of the same kinds of organisations which do not. (Hint — think of organisations which have gone out of business or were seen to be failing and taken over.)

Using the strategy of TQM to maintain customer service will entail:

- staff development and training to support commitment to quality

- a clear picture of current levels of quality

- shared ownership of problems

- shared commitment to change

- shared responsibility.

This requires an approach based on:

- top-down management

- total involvement

- full knowledge of customers and suppliers

- agreement on customer/supplier requirements

- agreement on ownership responsibilities.

Pareto analysis

This is based on the work of Pareto, who suggests that 80% of profit comes from 20% of customers. This analysis is then applied throughout organisations.

PANDA — *an acronym*

- **P**repare: define problem and establish root cause

- **A**ct: suggest positive action to measure criteria and generate solutions

- **N**avigate: chart planned route to define objectives and determine responsibilities

- **D**o: implement positive actions with measurable results

- **A**ssess: actively assess the actions taken and establish new standards as the solution.

Case study — customer service

One name that springs to mind as dominating our high streets for many years is Marks & Spencer. The company outsources much of its logistics work and demands very high standards. It grew from very small beginnings: two small traders coming together.

For many people it has become synonymous with quality in relation to the products it sells and its treatment of customers.

In many ways it was also seen as an indicator of how well the UK economy was performing. It remained a family firm for many years before going public. The management style was very much top-down, indeed it was often said to be 'autocratic'.

What could not be denied, however, was how committed top management was.

They would arrive individually or in small groups at the outlets, totally unannounced, then visit staff to ask how the goods and areas they had responsibility for were performing. An excellent communication system existed. If a new range of, say, ladies fashions had just been supplied to stores, within hours top management would be enquiring how things were going. If certain items were selling well in the Harrogate store but not in the Edinburgh store then the items in Edinburgh not selling well would be transferred to Harrogate. This was constant and ongoing!

Marks & Spencer established a number of practices that made customers continue to use them. For example:

- They are always on the high street or main thoroughfare

- They have an excellent customer return system — which means that you can return goods within a specific period as long as you produce your receipt. No questions are asked

- Their stores are always bright, clean and attractive places

- Their staff are well trained and fit the Marks & Spencer philosophy

- The products supplied are seen to be of good quality but at a reasonable price.

Self-Assessed Question

 2.5

What are the benefits for customers of the approaches adopted by organisations such as Marks & Spencer who have this total approach to quality?

Customer care standards

The British Standards Institute is the body officially charged with setting the standards to which those who produce goods or services must aspire. Its famous logo is a kite and where an item carries this logo it is deemed to have met the appropriate standard.

The key aspects of the standard are given in Figure 2.3; the customer is perceived to be the focal point.

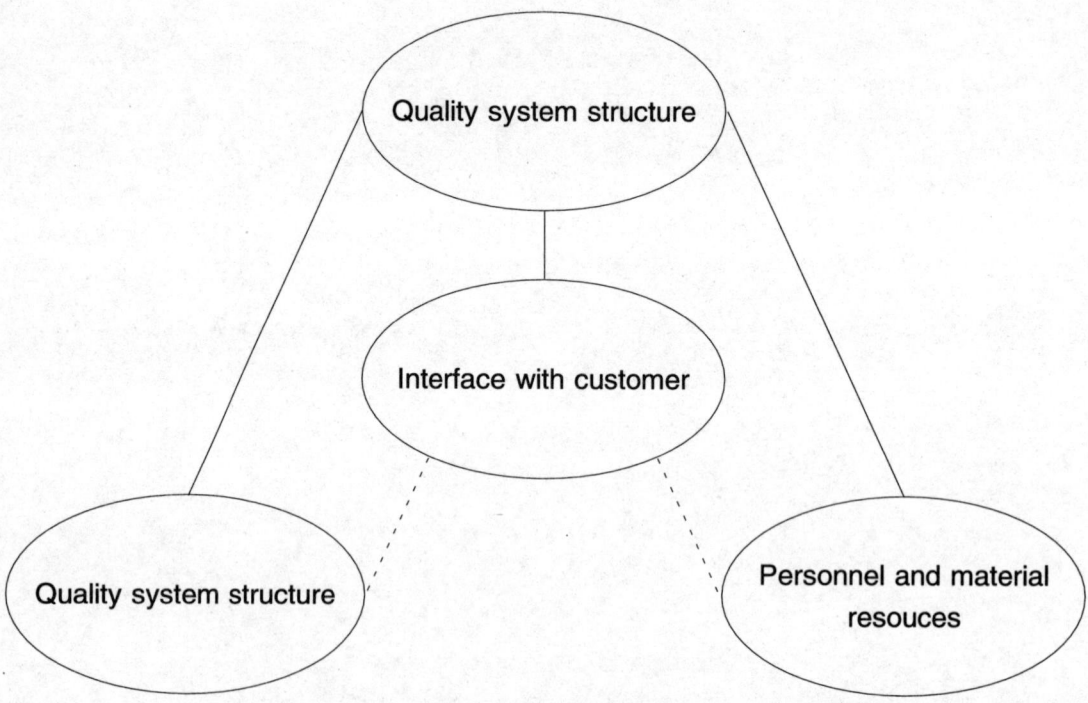

Figure 2.3 Key aspects of the British Standards.

Within this framework a range of characteristics are defined which may be:

- quantitative, i.e. measurable

- qualitative, i.e. comparable.

Quantitative aspects

This concept is based on numbers. You could, for example, check customers' records to see how many complaints have been received on goods or services and determine which ones are creating most customer dissatisfaction. For internal customers you might want to know where budgets or costs are being exceeded.

Qualitative aspects

Here the most important feature is the quality of service. Many firms now contact customers sometime after purchase of the service to specifically ask if all is well. You will appreciate too how vital quality is for internal customers because if they receive a good or service from their supplying department that is not up to specification they may have to return it, pushing up costs and causing delays.

Definition will depend on how evaluation takes place and whether the customer or service organisation does the evaluation.

To maintain quality standards in the logistics industry consider the following management responsibilities:

- the grade of service to be provided

- the service organisation's image and reputation for quality

- the objectives for service quality

- the approach to be adopted in pursuit of quality objectives

- the role of the company personnel responsible for implementing the quality policy

- continuous improvement of the service.

Self-Assessed Question

 2.4

List some service characteristics.

Customer delight

It is not possible to define absolutely what would delight your customers but the following may be considered:

- raising standards beyond those currently expected by customers so that they are genuinely gratified instead of merely satisfied

- introducing new forms of customer service in advance of customer expectations through service marketing.

An example of service marketing is the 'Tetley round tea bag tactic'. Tetley already had a large share of the tea market with their square tea bags. They introduced round tea bags, claiming they gave a rounder flavour and marketed them at a premium price. No consumer pressure had been established for round tea bags but customers were delighted with the new product and willingly paid the higher price.

Customer dissatisfaction	Customer satisfaction	Customer delight
←———————————————————————————→		
Imbalance of needs and expectations	Balance of needs and expectations	Customer expectations exceeded

A number of methods can be used to ensure that customer satisfaction levels are maintained.

Formal methods

- Surveys and questionnaires

- Customer comment cards

- Letters of complaint or commendation

- Structured conversations with customers

- Telephone polling.

Informal methods

- Obvious customer behaviour

- Noting customers who do not appear to be being served

- Body language

- Talking to customers

- Long queues

- Becoming a customer.

All organisations will rely on information received. What is required is:

- prompt information

- easy interpretation

- honest information

- encouragement of customers to provide real information

- help to establish cost-effective solutions.

Problems to be aware of in feedback:

- Written evidence may be weak particularly if created from anecdotes

- Is the customer response a big enough sample to evaluate and act upon?

- Have dissatisfied customers voted with their feet and not complained?

- Have certain customers who are seen as high status been given undue importance?

- Perception of service may be out of date. Are customers kept up to date with changes?

The last few years have seen a revolution in the methods used to record and store information. Even our telephone calls to organisations may be recorded and stored. This has the advantage of assisting with training of employees and dealing in facts when complaints are made.

It has also meant the ability to quickly search through databases, for example to extract customer information with accuracy and at a speed previously undreamt of.

The Internet has begun to change the business habits of many organisations. This will solve many problems but bring new ones.

For all these reasons and others given throughout this unit, it is increasingly clear that organisations which do not address the issue of customer care by continually reviewing their policies in this area, then comparing them with competitors and ensuring that they are continually empowering staff to establish positive relationships with customers, will falter and lose ground.

All of the following should be considered in designing a customer care strategy.

Not all seem, initially, to be geared to the needs of customers but, after some reflection, it should be obvious that any organisation in which these strategies are implemented will be at the forefront of customer satisfaction.

- Internal customer needs — high standard of product quality

- External customer needs — to be treated courteously

- Internal supplier needs — clear understanding of quality required

- Quality — get it right first time, every time

- Employee motivation — they want to do the job well

- Efficiency and control — things happen on time

- Customer satisfaction — feedback few complaints

- Achievement of targets — all output meets quality specification

- Reliable flow of goods/services — no delays from production through to delivery

- Change management — management system means fast response

- Financial issues — produced within budget to quality, on time.

5.4 Summary of this section

This section has addressed issues for the logistics industry relating to the care of customers. In a fast-growing global marketplace competition is fierce and companies need to be aware of the needs of both internal and external customers.

The elements of customer service have been identified, the contribution of customer service to buyer/supplier relationships explored and the customer service approach to logistics and distribution discussed.

5.5 Answers to SAQs

SAQ 2.1

1. Communication skills

2. Listening skills

3. Negotiation skills

SAQ 2.2

There is a difficulty in defining what we mean by customer satisfaction. You should now understand that it is 'customer perception'. This means that it is entirely the customer's decision whether or not he or she is satisfied with a product or the service provided.

You should, of course, be aware that there is a fine dimension to satisfaction. Imagine, for example, that you were completely satisfied with a product and the service you received which you purchased from a local firm. You go back to that same firm some months later but your experience is totally different.

Now you are a dissatisfied customer. You are particularly unhappy with the service you have received. Your perceptions are altered. Remember the continuum? You have moved from the point of balance on the continuum well towards that end which suggests dissatisfaction.

Remember too that we suggested that a loyal customer will probably be a satisfied customer who returns again and again to a company or firm because they judge the whole experience of purchasing from that firm to be always positive.

SAQ 2.3

- Is external customer feedback obtained?

- If it is, is it acted upon?

- Are staff trained and developed in best practice techniques and is that training ongoing?

- Do firms and companies grasp the message that 'quality' is determined by the customer?

You could perhaps say at this point that internal service quality impinges upon external service quality to obtain satisfied customers who are retained and loyal customers.

The thrust of this section is that only a satisfied or, better, a delighted customer will be a loyal customer. And the perception of that is entirely in the hands of the customer who will determine whether his/her perceived needs and expectations have been fully met!

SAQ 2.4

It is best to note that no organisation will adopt this approach for truly altruistic reasons. It is, quite simply, a drive towards profit maintenance. Happy, satisfied customers mean return business.

SAQ 2.5

- Quality

- Reliability

- Aftercare system

- Clarity of information

- Generally no-quibble attitude

- Well-trained knowledgeable staff

- Good environment.

5.6 Answers to activities

Activity 2.1

This activity can be used for individual learning or as part of a group activity.

The internal and external customers will depend on which organisation is being discussed.

Activity 2.2

Most people would want regular users and advocates.

Activity 2.3

No answer is provided for this activity as it essentially requires that each individual makes a list which applies only to them or involves organisations in a particular geographical area.

When the activity is completed the results could be used for a group discussion session.

Activity 2.4

- Waiting time

- Delivery time
- Hygiene, safety, reliability and security
- Responsiveness
- Accessibility
- Comfort
- Environmentally sound
- Competence
- State of the art
- Credibility
- Communication
- Process time.

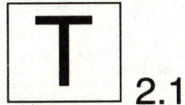 2.1

Tutor-marked assignment: Outcomes 1 and 2

You are asked to develop an outline which includes all of the points that you would consider to be important in:

1. the development of a basic management system for a large logistics company.

2. the identification of the elements of international systems.

3. key aspects and design of a customer care strategy for a medium-sized transport company.

6

Section 3: Operation of the major components of an international logistics network

6.1 Introduction to this section

What this section is about

This section is about inventory decisions in terms of the logistics network, transport decisions in terms of modal choice, combined transport and warehousing facilities relating to location, and automation.

Outcomes, aims and objectives

The aim is to describe the operation of the major components of the logistics industry.

Approximate study time

12 hours.

Other resources required

Access to the Internet, trade journals and newspapers would be helpful.

6.2 Assessment information for this section

How you will be assessed

As part of this unit Outcomes 3 and 4 are assessed by an extended-response question covering all the performance criteria for both outcomes (it may also be possible to assess the outcomes by means of a distribution plan). The case study scenario on which all assessment is based is printed at the end of Section 1. The questions are printed at the end of this section (Section 3) and the suggested solution is printed at the end of Section 4.

When and where you will be assessed

Assessment will take place at an appropriate point of study and at a place decided by tutors and centre staff.

What you have to achieve

Satisfactory completion of extended-response question covering all performance criteria.

Opportunities for reassessment

Normally, you will be given one attempt to pass an assessment with one reassessment opportunity.

Your centre will also have a policy covering 'exceptional' circumstances, for example if you have been ill for an extended period of time. Each case will be considered on an individual basis and is at your centre's discretion (usually via written application), and they will decide whether or not to allow a third attempt. Please contact your tutor for details regarding how to apply.

6.3 Logistics decisions: elements of the logistics network

There are many parts to logistics networks so before returning to the component parts to describe their operation it will be helpful to remind ourselves of some of the services, features and benefits that a large logistics company would be hoping to provide for customers, incorporate into the company management and gain from good practice and effective strategic management.

Services show activities which will form part of internal partnerships in integrated companies or the benefits that can be gained from outsourcing parts of the operation to specialist companies. Features list the service levels that customers can expect and benefits show the rewards for the company.

Services

- Product warehousing

- Inventory management

- Pack and ship

- Custom packaging, invoicing and promotional documentation

- Returns management

- Transportation management

- Custom reporting

- Value-added services (such as marketing inserts and gift wrapping)

- Kitting and assembly

- Serial number capture

- Warranty management

- Administration

- Import/export expertise.

Features

- Variety/multiple delivery options: next-day, ground, postal

- Extended hours for same-day shipping

- Automated picking and high volume capabilities

- Many quality checks and audit procedures

- On-site security and inventory protection.

Benefits

- High level of accuracy in enhanced customer satisfaction

- Faster order completion

- Lower inventory costs, direct costs and overhead costs

- Flexible warehouse planning.

In attempting to operate an efficient logistics operation three of the main elements to be addressed are:

a) inventory decisions

b) transport decisions

c) warehousing facilities.

Inventory decisions

Inventory control is, basically, about how much stock is stored at any one time and how it is kept track of. It applies to every item used to produce at every stage of the production process (from purchase through to delivery).

The terms 'stock control' and 'inventory control' are used in this unit to mean exactly the same thing.

Stock can tie up a large amount of business capital, so accurate information about stock levels and values is essential for good accounting. Good control means that the right amount of stock is in the right place at the right time, ensuring that capital is not tied up unnecessarily and that production is protected when there are problems with the supply chain.

Inventory control is concerned with minimising the total cost of inventory (in the UK inventory control is regularly referred to as stock control. The reason for using both terms is to avoid confusion for anyone reading text books from the USA, where the term 'inventory' is used, or Europe, where the term 'stock' is used).

There are three main features to inventory control decision making, each of which is very important in logistics. They are:

1. cost of holding stock;

2. cost of placing an order;

3. cost of a shortage.

A trading firm has stock in the form of goods for resale. Companies operating in logistics networks will have stock in the form of direct materials, work in progress and finished goods.

Managers often have to make decisions about stock level over a very limited period. This would be the case over a holiday period when stocks of sun-care products need to satisfy demand over the limited holiday dates.

As such products have 'use before' dates they will have almost no value if retained to the next holiday period. Of course if there is an unusually hot summer and the products are understocked there is a potential profit loss.

To summarise, businesses hold stocks in a variety of forms:

- work in progress

- raw materials

- finished goods

- plant and machine spares

- consumables.

The aim is to have enough stock to meet customers', as well as companies', needs. Having too high or too low stock is harmful.

Effects of too low a stock	Effects of too high a stock
It may be impossible to satisfy consumer demands	Risk of obsolete stock
Loss of business	High stock losses
Loss of goodwill	Ties up working capital
Frequent ordering, leading to higher handling costs	High storage costs

Sometimes companies build up buffer stocks as a way of guaranteeing that they do not run out of stock if the demand for products increases. This is a risky business. If the forecast is right, i.e. there is demand for the stockpiled stock, then profits will be made. If, however, there is a downturn in demand the stock will be a very costly asset.

Stock levels

Maximum stock: the most stock that the firm is willing

or able to hold.

Minimum stock: this is the stock below which it is felt to be unsafe for the firm to operate.

Re-order level: the point at which the firm will re-order stock.

Re-order quantity: this is the number of new items that will be bought in when stocks fall to the re-order level if there is an unexpected variation in demand. When this applies a minimum level will be set.

Supply of items '**just in time**' for their immediate use is the objective of all stock planning systems.

Pull systems refer to a group of techniques that aim to ensure that when stock is used it is replaced. Pull systems do not plan, they react. They will work fine if processes and logistics are infinitely flexible, do not vary and are uncomplicated.

Pull techniques generally use visual controls rather than computer systems. In their simplest form they mean replacement, i.e. simply replacing a used item.

Push systems are systems in which orders are made for everything likely to be needed. The obvious disadvantage is that it is difficult to forecast all of the time.

For items that are likely to be in short supply in the future, and are of low value, this may be the obvious solution.

Last in first out (LIFO) means that where there is more than one of a particular item the last one received is sold first. This implies that the newest is the most expensive.

First in first out (FIFO) means that where there is more than one of a particular item the first one received is sold first. This means that stock is rotated.

Self-Assessed Question

 3.1

Inventory control involves controlling stock levels by keeping track of them at every stage from purchase to delivery.

What would you list as being stock?

The amount of stock to be kept at any one given time will be dependent on what type of stock it is. The following case study illustrates the importance of good systems:

Case study: Leverage Logistics Solutions

Jennifer Taylor is the managing director of Leverage Logistics Solutions. The business specialises in speedy 'day after' deliveries of recycled computer print cartridges. To control stock the company has invested in an integrated computerised accounting system. The system has capacity to deal with stock control, buying, on-going costs, etc. The main attraction of the system is that it offers barcoding. Each item is barcoded as soon as it comes to the company and thus it is logged into the system under a purchase order with a serial number, stock code and product detail. The system can tell exactly where each item is in the warehouse and whether or not cartridges have gone through the recycling process.

When it comes to the number of cartridges not yet processed it is impossible to keep to rigid stock levels. People want to send cartridges for recycling when it is convenient for them. If it is not possible to recycle them the cartridges are not purchased so there will be some stockpiling before they are sold on.

When it comes to consumables such as office stationery it is a different matter. Such things are only purchased when necessary or when there is a special offer.

Jennifer has installed a computer connection at home. She can access stock levels at all times and bid for products from home, if necessary. She can also keep abreast of any health or safety issues such as when there might be hazardous materials in the warehouse.

Activity

 3.1

It is obvious from the case study that different inventory control methods may be used depending on what is being purchased.

Using library, web or book resources research what is meant by the following terms:

- minimum stock level

- stock review

- just in time

- re-order lead time

- economic order quantity

- batch control

- first in, first out.

Self-Assessed Question

 3.2

Are there any health and safety aspects to stock control?

Stock control is very much linked to the overall costs in the logistics industry. With high costs involved in storage and transportation it is essential that the right levels are maintained. Very important decisions regarding transportation and warehousing costs will be crucial.

As mentioned in other parts of this unit, supply chain integration is part of modern thinking for both logistics service providers and users, and buyers of logistics services. The end-to-end integrated supply chain is an ideal where the entire chain is transparent to the customer, providing opportunities for collaboration between buyers, sellers and carriers in strategic planning, forecasting and stock control.

Increased collaboration with logistics providers offers opportunities for effective and efficient measures to monitor and control stock/inventory levels.

Transport decisions

One very important issue for transportation is that governments are getting out of the transport business. Mostly they do not now view this as a core government activity. This is linked to the loss of public services, and the global and local roles for transport, with most effect in passenger transport.

In the UK, as in most economies, the government is

very much involved in policy making for future road building.

Current thinking calls for research into integrating/linking/enhancing rail, road and inland waterways in an attempt to curb the extension of road transport.

This calls for forward-looking engineering projects allowing for the integration of the transport system. Much of the finance for this type of activity is likely to be met through public finance (perhaps linked, in part, to private finance initiatives).

Meanwhile, privatised providers are mainly accountable to shareholders. This often means that there is pressure to return high profit, sometimes from constantly reducing costs.

This situation is very obvious where in some countries public bus companies have been replaced by thousands of single operators (sometimes in passenger transport the trend for huge companies is stalled for a while after de-regulation). Rail operators have, increasingly, met the same fate and many seaports are operated for the advantage of shareholders.

Each country will be different but, in the main, over the past few years transport has been handed over to international transport companies and supply chain managers.

National transport planning (logistics planning) is no longer appropriate and is now dealt with through local and international competition between private commercial interests. Mergers and alliances are very important to transport operators as they view future ability to provide global solutions as vital to survival.

Transport is an industry in growth. It is also an industry placed under great demand pressure. Resulting air and road congestion are unlikely to be dealt with solely by market forces, nor will environmental standards be protected or safety and security standards guaranteed. Public and governmental involvement continues to be necessary; it is just that the focus has changed.

It is interesting to note that major airlines are continuing to work in alliances. Information about some of these alliances can be found at:

- *www.oneworldalliance.com*

- *www.skyteam.com*

- *www.star-alliance.com*

Self-Assessed Question

 3.3

List some areas in the transportation industries which have been privatised over the past 20 years.

Self-Assessed Question

 3.4

Name some alliances made by airlines in an attempt to have global alliances.

Transport companies are increasingly becoming both international and inter-modal with investments running through shipping, ports, road transport and rail transport. Airline alliances and international container shipping companies operate their global networks between key airport and port hubs from where they pick up feeder traffic.

A large part of current transport infrastructure investment is focussed on large port terminals or massive airports. Competition to raise the funds, equipment and operational skills necessary to compete is fierce.

Rail operators such as the high-speed European rail consortium Thalys are making ticket arrangements with airlines such as American Airlines to operate inter-modal global route networks.

It is important to know the difference between inter-modal transport and multimodal transport (sometimes referred to as combined transport).

Inter-modal transport involves movement of goods in one loading unit or vehicle which uses successively a few methods of transport, without the goods themselves actually being handled.

Multimodal, or combined, transportation involves transportation of goods by at least two means of transportation. The main reason for needing to know this distinction is that in the UK the collection of transport statistics is mostly based on modal activity.

Global sea freight port operators are buying into key port hubs in other countries.

There is a well-financed, well-organised lobby of the transport industry, including operators, freight forwarders and logistics companies whose aim is to ensure that when new international or regional standards are set they are advantageous to members.

This has implications for regulatory barriers, some of which have been effective while others have simply hindered global transportation. There is also great pressure on the World Trade Organisation to promote the opening of transport markets.

This restructuring of the world's transport systems is all about providing for the delivery of volume commodities at high speed. The industry appears to have become fragmented into specialised providers offering services such as security, maintenance, loading, etc.

Having helped the process of trans-national opportunities in other industries, the industry is going through the process itself. Huge amounts of foreign direct investment funding aids are directed towards transport industries. This is not without its problems. Many of these were included in the article addressing the logistics industry in Section 1.

Many studies worldwide are currently underway to rationalise transport networks and provide solutions to sustainable transportation. An item, printed below, from the Australian Institute of Petroleum highlights the issue of fuel consumption from derivatives of fossil fuel.

The 'green' logistics issue in Section 5 re-visits this ever important issue for the logistics industry.

Alternative transport fuels

At present, about 80% of the world's demand for transportation fuels — road, rail, air and sea — is met by derivatives from the fossil fuel petroleum. Petrol, one of the major derivatives of petroleum, is used throughout the world as a motor vehicle fuel.

Other petroleum derivatives, including diesel and liquid petroleum gas, can be used in motor vehicles as alternatives to petrol as can compressed natural gas, which often occurs in conjunction with petroleum deposits.

Some alternatives are derived from non-fossil, or partly renewable, sources such as grain or other agricultural crops. However, these need fertilisers made from fossil fuels, etc. and are not, therefore, totally renewable.

The major fossil fuel alternatives to petrol are:

- diesel

- liquid petroleum gas (LPG)

- compressed natural gas (CNG)

- ethers — methyl tertiary butyl ether (MTBE) produced from natural gas and butane

- electricity from coal/oil/gas

- methanol produced from natural gas or coal.

The major non-fossil alternative fuels are:

- ethanol

- hydrogen.

Although about eight million vehicles worldwide currently run on blends containing alternative fuels, it is unlikely that any one of these fuels will achieve the worldwide usage of petrol in the foreseeable future, primarily because they are too expensive.

However, the concerns about the impact of fossil fuels on the environment is driving the quest for suitable alternatives.

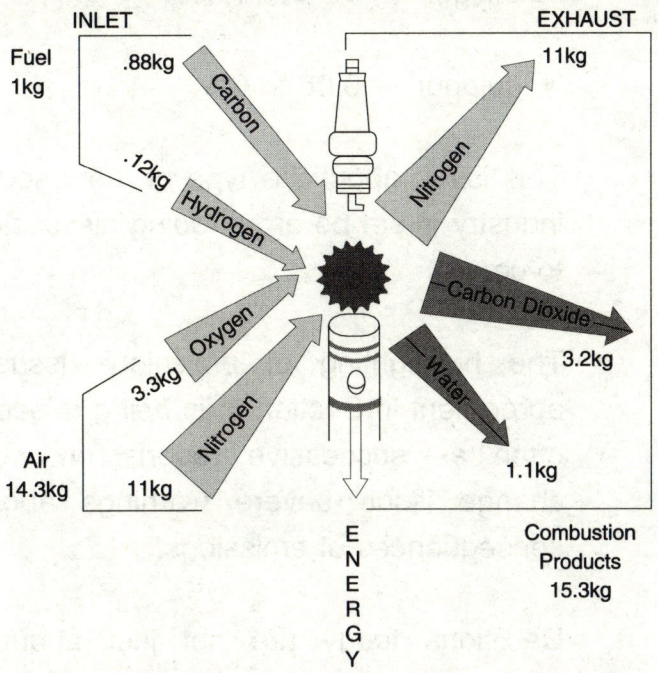

Petroleum

Petroleum, which is also called crude oil, is found in underground deposits throughout the world and contains up to 300 compounds of hydrogen and carbon, or hydrocarbons, as well as sulphur and nitrogen. Its elemental composition is fairly constant:

- carbon — 83 to 87%

- hydrogen — 10 to 14%

- nitrogen — 0.1 to 2%

- oxygen — 0.05 to 1.5%

- sulphur — 0.05 to 6%

This issue about the type of fuel used in the transport industry is set be an on-going discussion topic in years to come.

The highlighting of emissions issues (see Kyoto agreement in Section 5) is being raised more and more often as successive reports on worldwide climate change issue severe warnings about the possible consequences of emissions.

Decisions today are not just about the modes of transport, routes to be taken, stocks and costs. Increasingly questions relating to the environment are of significant importance.

(Source: http://www.world-petroleum.org/education/atfuels/index.html)

Self-Assessed Question

3.5

Transport systems have allowed industries to globalise. Are there any problems for the globalisation of the transport industry?

Self-Assessed Question

 3.6

State the difference between modal choice and combined transport.

Transport issues are very much at the forefront of discussions as to how best to accommodate the growth of the movement of goods.

National governments, unions such as the European Union (EU) and trade organisations such as the World Trade Organisation address the requirements and issues raised by the growth of logistics.

The following update was provided in September 2006. It was issued by the EU and entitled *Europa — Overviews of the European Activities — Transport.*

Open frontiers and affordable transport have given Europeans unprecedented levels of personal mobility. Goods are shipped rapidly and efficiently from factory to customer, often in different countries. The European Union (EU) has contributed by opening national markets to competition and by removing physical and technical barriers to free movement. But today's transport patterns and growth rates are unsustainable.

The ability to move people and goods quickly, efficiently and cheaply is a central tenet of the EU's goal for a dynamic economy and cohesive society. The transport sector generates 10% of EU wealth measured by gross domestic product (GDP), equivalent to about one trillion euro a year. It provides more than 10 million jobs.

The removal of barriers to cross-border trade and

travel has increased the volume of long-distance goods and passenger transport. This phenomenon is being repeated in the wake of the 2004 EU enlargement with significant increases, particularly of road freight, between the new members and the rest of the Union.

The constant growth in mobility puts severe strains on transport systems. Congestion on roads and at airports increases pollution, adding an estimated 6% to EU fuel consumption.

The need for common action

Although many aspects of transport policy come under national governments, it makes sense for the European single market to have a single transport infrastructure. In the last 10 years, the EU has opened national transport markets across the Union to competition, particularly in the road and air sectors and, to a lesser extent, for rail.

As a result, trucks can operate in countries other than their own, so that they no longer return empty on international journeys.

The liberalisation of air travel has brought more competition and lower fares as well as more connections between member states. In March 2003, a first package of measures to liberalise rail infrastructure took effect, opening about 70 – 80% of rail freight traffic over main lines to competition.

The EU also promotes major transport infrastructure projects, the so-called Trans-European Networks (TENs). Among the priority TENs projects are:

- the removal of bottlenecks on the main east-west inland waterway linking the Rhine, Main and Danube

- a programme to regulate traffic on the busy shipping lanes off the EU coasts

- several north-south and east-west rail upgrades.

A balancing act

Liberalisation alone has not been able to solve several deep-seated problems. Besides congestion, these include the dominance of road over other forms of transport, pollution, and the fragmentation of transport systems, including poor links to outlying regions or the lack of good connections between regional or national networks.

Road haulage now carries 44% of all goods transported in the EU, against 41% for short-sea shipping routes, 8% for rail and 4% for inland waterways. The imbalance is more marked for passenger transport where road (largely car journeys) accounts for 79% against rail's 6% and 5% for air. Shifting goods and passengers from roads to less polluting forms of transport will be a key factor in any sustainable transport policy. Another will be the ability to integrate different modes of transport by combining road-rail, sea-rail or rail-air elements.

Congestion charging, where users pay for the scarce infrastructure they occupy on roads, at airports or elsewhere, is also being introduced. One example is the system put in place in London in 2003 which charges motorists for driving into the city's central district. Pilot programmes for similar systems are in place in several other major cities.

In a democratic market economy, a switch from road to rail (however desirable) cannot be imposed by the EU or implemented by government fiat. It is best done through a process of incentives, like targeted investments in other transport modes so that they can handle the overflow, and pricing schemes which reflect the real cost of road use and which encourage a 'natural' migration from roads to alternative forms of transport.

The purpose is to have fewer long-distance passengers or goods travelling by road and more by rail, and to replace some short-haul passenger flights by rail journeys.

Paying for pollution

Figure 3.1   Waterborne transport has a bigger role to play in moving goods to market.

Infrastructure charging also supports the idea of paying for pollution caused. The transport sector, principally road vehicles, is responsible for about 28% of all EU emissions of CO_2, the main greenhouse gas.

Better fuel efficiency, the use of alternative fuels and fuel taxation are all measures being introduced.

In the air transport sector, the inevitable expansion of airport capacities needs to be linked to new regulations to reduce noise and emissions caused by aircraft.

In the wake of oil spills like those of the *Erika* and the *Prestige* off the French and Spanish coasts, the European Commission is pressing for more rules on maritime safety, including tougher ship inspections, sanctions for pollution caused through gross negligence, and the accelerated phasing out of single-hulled tankers. Since these disasters, the Commission also publishes a list of sub-standard ships banned from EU ports, which is updated on a regular basis.

In another safety move, the European Commission published in March 2006 for the first time a list of 92 airlines which are banned from operating passenger or freight flights to or from EU airports. Most of the banned airlines are based in Africa.

Action plan

In a 2001 White Paper on transport, the Commission set goals for each sector, some of which are already being implemented. For instance, the Council of Ministers reached agreement in June 2004 to increase the compulsory rest periods for drivers of heavy trucks from 8 to 9 hours and to limit their total driving time per week to 56 hours.

This is part of a wider safety programme to cut road deaths, currently more than 40,000 a year, by half by 2010. The other White Paper targets seek to:

- reverse the decline in rail's share of passenger and freight transport. A freight train in the EU travels at an average speed of 18 kilometres per hour. Rail must improve speeds and service levels if it is to attract freight traffic from roads

- reduce flight delays by creating an integrated European air traffic control structure

- invest more in maritime and inland waterways. Improve port services and maritime safety standards

- mix modes to offer greater efficiency, less congestion, lower costs and cleaner air. Introduce integrated ticketing and baggage handling for dual mode journeys.

In a review of transport policy in June 2006, the European Commission said the short-term focus of the action plan should now be on making railways more competitive, introducing a ports policy, developing intelligent transport systems, charging for infrastructure use, producing more bio-fuels and looking at ways to make towns and cities less congested.

This article offers a particularly European perspective but will highlight similar problems and issues to those raised in other highly developed high-volume transport areas worldwide.

The last paragraph is particularly worth taking note of.
In fact, the European Commission plans to initiate a number of actions. These will include:

a) Optimisation of existing transport modes

  ○ An internal market review of road transport to ensure the proper functioning of the market, determine the role of small — medium business enterprises (SMEs) and provide an analysis of the social elements involved

  ○ Launch European ports policy (2007)

  ○ Removal of technical barriers in rail transport to ensure interoperability between companies. Programme to promote rail freight corridors and prepare a review of the internal market in rail transport, with a scoreboard for market performance of rail (2007)

  ○ A review of air transport liberalisation measures, airport charges and capacity

  ○ A mobilisation of all sources of infrastructure financing: multi — annual investment programme up to 2013 for trans-European networks.

b) Mobility of the citizen

  ○ Publication of a Green Paper on Urban Transport (2007)

  ○ Development of a strategy for critical infrastructure,

land and public transport security (2007), and review air and maritime security rules (2008)

- Passenger rights: proposal on minimum standards for coach transport, notably for people with limited mobility (2007)

- A first European road safety day (2007): promotion of road safety through vehicle design and technology, infrastructure and drive behaviour (ongoing basis)

- Review legislation on working conditions in the road sector (2007).

c) Better transport solutions through new technologies

- Development of freight transport logistics strategy, as well as the launch of broad debate on possible preparation of an EU action plan for 2007

- Energy and transport: strategic technology plan for energy in 2007 and green propulsion programme for 2009.

One area that is often overlooked in the discussion of moving freight across land is the importance of internal waterways.

Strategic transport policies in the UK have not placed much emphasis on the use of internal waterways. In

19th century Britain much of the transport investment was in rail networks, thus allowing canals to decline in terms of volume of freight.

The cost of loading and unloading waterway shipments tends to be higher than for other modes of transport.

Self-Assessed Question

 3.7

We are now familiar with many of the types of goods that would be transported.

1. What types of goods might be transported by inland waterway?

2. What might the advantages of using the waterways be?

Inland Navigation Europe (INE) is an organisation that looks at, amongst other things, the feasibility of trans-European transport networks, including waterways. It regards inland shipping issues. Currently, investment in waterway infrastructure is a public issue. This is because waterways development covers tourism, flood protection, energy power and nature conservation as well as transport issues.

However, the organisation points out that investment projects in the transport sector have a life of many decades for the benefit of future generations. Long-term gain is very significant for waterways projects.

INE claims that the establishment of a European Transport Observatory is a necessity if the enlarged EU is to develop a strategic, trans-European network.
INE is included in this part of the text to show that waterway development is being seriously considered in the EU. There will be similar types of initiative taking place in other national and international trading blocks.

Activity

3.2

Read the following article, reprinted from *Transport International*, 11 April 2003.

The objective of this activity is to familiarise yourself with key issues identified by the World Trade Organisation as they relate to the transport/logistics industry.

Transport: The WTO's Problem Industry

The World Trade Organisation (WTO) was set up by governments in 1995 as a successor to the post-war trade body the General Agreement on Tariffs and Trade (GATT) to drive forward an unending agenda of global market liberalisation. Not only commercial industries have been affected. Even basic services such as water supply and public transport are being opened up to international market forces in a ratchet-like process, which obliges member states to enter 'successive negotiations' for more and more liberalisation.

Key among the visions of global industry is a seamless global transport system. Yet while individual transport sectors continue to liberalise, the WTO has made little progress in bringing transport under the influence of its own services framework — the General Agreement on Trade in Services, or GATS. This is something the WTO is determined to change.

Among trade unions' concerns about the growing power of the WTO is its refusal to consider the incorporation of international core labour standards into its rules for trade in both goods and in services. Unlike other international organisations such as the International Civil Aviation Organisation, the WTO has no form of stakeholder dialogue. Global unions, including the ITF, are therefore pressing demands both for some form of consultative status in the WTO, and for vital restrictions on its remit, particularly when it comes to public services.

In the meantime transport industries continue to throw up complex challenges and obstacles to the WTO campaign.

Maritime talks run aground

International shipping has long operated in an environment of global deregulation. There are few restrictions on ships carrying cargo from one country to another. Shipping has produced its own extreme strain of deregulation, the flag of convenience system, which places a large part of the industry beyond the influence of government control.

Barriers remain, however, in many domestic shipping services. Most genuine flag states insist that, in line with UN rules, there must be a genuine link between the shipowner and the flag state. There are therefore restrictions on foreign ownership and national laws, including labour laws, apply on board. In some countries foreign ships are banned from coastal trade (cabotage). One of these countries is the USA, where the US Jones Act allows only US flagged ships whose crews enjoy US conditions to transport goods internally.

Talks began on shipping and port services as soon as GATS was set up in 1995, but these collapsed when the US government rejected any challenge to the rules reserving its coastal trade to national shipping. The USA has since made it clear that access to its domestic market is non-negotiable, and following 11 September 2001 sensitivity over coastal and port security has virtually ensured that eliminating cabotage will stay off the agenda.

But maritime transport includes much more than domestic shipping services and the negotiating freeze has created enormous frustration among the growing number of global terminal operators, such as Hong Kong-based Hutchison, which is the largest international port and terminal operator in the world. There was little surprise in March 2001 when the Hong Kong government urged an early resumption of maritime talks in order to discuss the elimination of restrictions on foreign equity ownership and management in ports.

The aviation exclusion

Civil aviation is even more problematic for the WTO than maritime transport. Air traffic services have been specifically excluded from GATS since the outset, due to the political and economic sensitivity surrounding air links from one country to another. The WTO's other problem in its struggle for influence is that an effective international framework of rules for air traffic rights already exists.

The 1944 Chicago Convention, overseen by the International Civil Aviation Organisation (ICAO), a UN specialised agency, provides a legal framework for more than 3000 negotiated bilateral air agreements. It is also a regulatory regime, which keeps safety, security and economic and environmental regulation under one roof.

The ICAO system of bilaterals is derided as 'a nightmare' by former WTO Director General Mike Moore. Yet for years it has been the effective means by which a balanced exchange of market access has been achieved between any two countries under a principle of mutual benefit, rather than simply clearing the field for the giant carriers to dominate air services around the world. If traffic rights were brought within the scope of GATS, it would mean in principle that each country would have to offer all other WTO members the terms of its most liberal bilateral agreement.

The WTO cannot ignore ICAO but it has set out to go round it, absorb it, pressure it, and challenge it all at the same time. There are ongoing moves towards bringing air cargo out of the ICAO system and under GATS, despite the complication, repeatedly highlighted by the ITF among others, that most air cargo is carried in the bellies of passenger aircraft. In the meantime ICAO tries to keep the WTO at bay by pursuing its own aggressive programmes of liberalisation. A special ICAO conference scheduled for March 2003 appears ready to propose a further raft of liberalisation.

Once more the position of the USA in all this is problematic for the WTO. The USA has fiercely promoted the liberalisation of international air routes. However, the US domestic market — the largest aviation market in the world — provides a vital economic platform for its own aviation and aerospace industries. For this reason, the US government argues for 'open skies' agreements on international routes, but maintains a protective barrier around its domestic aviation market. For this arrangement to continue air traffic rights must stay outside the GATS framework.

While air traffic rights (what the WTO calls 'hard rights') are the key tradeable service in aviation, there are other important 'soft' areas of aviation business. It is unique to civil aviation, among all the services covered by GATS, that three areas of activity are specifically included in its remit. These are: aircraft repair (though not line maintenance); computer reservations and marketing. Yet the number of commitments made under GATS in these areas is paltry. In March 2002, out of 138 WTO member states, just three had made commitments on aircraft maintenance.

The widest category of aviation activities referred to (though excluded from) GATS is 'services directly related to air traffic services'. Inevitably this category is proving highly vulnerable to WTO tactics of redefinition and re-categorisation. This time the European Commission is leading the way on the WTO's behalf. Through the current round of talks, the Commission has simply moved airline catering out of the aviation industry (which is outside GATS) and reclassified it as part of the catering industry (inside GATS). The same has been done with professional crew training, which is now part of education services. The European Commission also wants commitments from countries to liberalise airport ground services under GATS after making a unilateral decision that these are not 'directly related to air traffic rights.

Logistics: side-stepping the blockages

A renewed push for shipping and port liberalisation is coming from the logistics companies. There is increasing concern that the GATS approach to global transport through different transport service sectors has not adapted to take account of recent developments in intermodal transport and logistics. Logistics deals not just with transport but with such matters as cargo handling, warehousing, customs clearance, container depots, and inventory management.

The Hong Kong government has pinpointed an indispensable need 'to meet the ever-increasing demand for customised door-to-door logistics services'. This position, which has strong support from the European Commission and the International Chambers of Commerce, is that maritime talks in GATS should put coastal trade issues to one side and move on to deal with the movement of goods through the ports and inland.

Failing the restart of maritime negotiations, the fall-back position would be to create a new service category for GATS called logistics services and set up a new negotiating group.

This approach links closely with the strategy being adopted by air cargo companies. Air courier companies such as UPS, Federal Express and others, in addition to lobbying to loosen the links between the ICAO system and air cargo operations, have also been pressing for the liberalisation of national postal services. To deal with this issue the WTO classified postal services and couriers within the same negotiating group. The cargo companies, aware of the high level of resistance to liberalising domestic postal services, now see themselves trapped in a negotiating group going nowhere fast. After huge corporate pressure, in July 2002 the US government proposed the setting up of a new separate GATS service sector called Express Delivery Services.

Not only maritime and aviation services are feeling the influence of the logistics lobby, but also road and rail further down the logistics chain. According to the International Chambers of Commerce: "It is recognised that land transport services may raise particularly sensitive issues. Nevertheless, given the growing significance of door-to-door services, inland transport (where it forms part of international maritime services) should be liberalised." A few governments, such as the UK, are ready to make binding commitments in the current round of GATS, which will ensure that their current policy of allowing foreign investment in rail is irreversible. The current process of rail liberalisation in Europe is already anticipating the inland march of GATS.

The current round

The WTO has failed in the current round of negotiations to make significant progress in the two areas of transport with truly global route networks. Yet the WTO is unlikely to give up on bringing all transport sectors into the GATS. The international and regional institutions, including the OECD, the World Bank and the European Commission, work together closely to promote diverse routes to the same goal of global liberalisation. They are backed by powerful new business lobbying groups representing the logistics and supply chain interests of the global corporations.

The organised pressure being mounted for transport liberalisation can seem overwhelming. Yet pollution and safety disasters constantly fuel public concerns about the impact of liberalisation. A renewed interest in security now shares the international political agenda with lowering trade barriers. There is also a wide range of powerful national economic interests at play, which are often in conflict with the WTO model of liberalisation.

If trade unions can get used to the new terrain, there is still plenty of scope for labour to pose a sustainable development alternative to the WTO's agenda of global free market liberalisation. Transport is still the WTO's problem industry.

What are the WTO and GATS?

The World Trade Organisation (WTO) was set up in 1995 following a prolonged round of international trade talks known as the Uruguay Round of the General Agreement on Tariffs and Trade (GATT). It was created with new powers to provide a permanent legal and administrative framework for the process of multilateral trade liberalisation.

The General Agreement on Trade in Services (GATS) is the framework under which trade in services is liberalised. This includes such basic services as water supply, telecommunications, postal services, energy services, health provision and transport. Hundreds of millions of workers are employed in these industries.

WTO negotiations work by bringing trade ministers together to discuss how much they are prepared to open their markets to each other. This process is pushed forward in timetabled rounds of negotiations. These talks operate in only one direction — the removal of trade barriers, and the extension of liberalisation.

The WTO also has certain important liberalisation principles which are enforced across all industries. These include:

- the national treatment principle — countries are not allowed to keep any measures which favour national businesses over foreign operators

and

- the most favoured nation principle — once a government has made a commitment it is offered equally to all other WTO member states.

Any country which fails to comply with its commitments is subject to substantial legally enforceable constraints backed up by trade sanctions. These mechanisms bind future governments and make liberalisation effectively irreversible.

Some key union concerns

- GATS free market aims can be in conflict with principles of universal or affordable access to basic services. This poses a serious threat to particular services including health, education and public transport. The ITF believes these services should be excluded from GATS

- Any form of regulation protecting the environment, health and safety and employee rights is vulnerable to being ruled illegal by the WTO as an 'unnecessary' or 'discriminatory' trade barrier. The WTO has refused to accept union proposals for international core labour standards to be incorporated into its rules

- WTO rules open the door to foreign companies insisting on market access to any services where some form of competition already exists. This would currently include most of the transport industries in most countries. The ITF, with its experience of flags of convenience in the maritime industry, believes governments must be able to retain national ownership rules and rules ensuring the application of national conditions

- GATS negotiations operate in an environment of secrecy and without the participation of key stakeholders. The ITF calls for transparency in the WTO and structures of social dialogue with industry stakeholders.

Warehousing decisions

Determining warehousing facilities which are consistent

with customer needs will mainly come down to decisions about where to locate and how to operate. Most systems will be automated.

To start to consider these two main decisions, first of all read the Mandoris case study.

Case study: Mansoris Ltd

Mansoris offers supply chain solutions which provide the best possible base for effective collaboration between a company, its customers and buyers.

It was set up to manage serious problems such as slow-moving stock and products with irregular demand. The solutions offered help distributors to maintain efficiency and speed in the chain.

Provision of advanced statistical analysis and probability planning allows for determination of ideal levels of stock for any situation, allowing for instant response to unexpectedly high or low periods of demand.

Solutions will also optimise inventories according to service level agreements.

Mandoris solutions also support new technologies in the warehouse management systems arena of supply chain management, helping to manage the movement of goods both inside and outside the organisation.

Warehouse tasks can be managed without time delay by using radio frequency data collection devices carried by warehouse operatives. The use of technology will show productivity gains because of improved inventory and order fulfilment accuracy.

The solutions offered are compliant with Electronic Data Interchange (EDI) standards.

Note: EDIs are discussed fully in Section 5.

Self-Assessed
Question

 3.8

What are the most obvious points about warehousing in the Mandoris case study?

Automation is necessary if goods flow is to be achieved at minimum cost. In the case study (Mandors) it was clear that radio frequency devices were being used for efficient warehousing solutions.

Voice technology is one of the most up-to-date methods used for order picking, receipt of goods and stock taking. This system uses speech recognition and speech synthesis to allow warehouse workers to communicate verbally with the system.

They use a headset that includes a microphone linked to a server by way of a radio frequency network.

The real advantage of this is that everything is done in current time; there are no delays in communication. Improvements in order picking will be significant.

Training time for new operators is short and paperwork/administration costs are reduced in monetary and time values.

Warehousing management is changing towards an emphasis on maximum efficiency product flow and cost management. These changes have come about as a result of the customer demand for fast, accurate deliveries.

Organising warehouse space and product flow is essential as is the need to minimise labour costs. It is not efficient to have employees manually pick up orders and store materials.

It is also becoming more common for there to be integration of customer order management and logistics operators, with incoming orders being directed to the most appropriate company.

Location would be a significant question for anyone setting up warehousing facilities. It is also a crucial question for any business setting up a new operation or a new section of an existing operation.

Activity

 3.2

Consider the points that may be taken into consideration by an entrepreneur about to set up a large warehousing facility.

Where transport is of importance in location decisions it will be so because a good transport system opens up new markets. It is usually the case that transport costs are influential but are not the main point considered when locating businesses on a national or international scale.

Increased speed and complexity of distribution networks has resulted in more companies outsourcing many of their transport functions to specialist firms.

This may mean that direct transport considerations are less important than they once were in location decisions.

Globalisation of the business environment means that it is increasingly important to consider national transport systems as a whole, and how they can connect with the rest of the world. Transport systems, or networks, are now viewed in relation to their proximity to transport hubs: air, sea, internal waterways or rail.

Heavy industries are likely to have the highest transport costs and, therefore, are more dependent on location.

As logistics firms develop their distribution networks to incorporate practices such as 'just in time' delivery, reliability of the transport network is the prime consideration.

Air transport appears to be the system which has the greatest influence on foreign investors and business services, whereas road transport has the largest influence on domestic investment. Businesses are now tending to move away from large cities to urban fringes.

High-technology manufacturing and service businesses often locate to the same geographical locations.

The environment in which businesses operate is complex and ever-changing. Business decisions will be taken to meet the needs at a particular time.

6.4 Summary of this section

This section has described the operation of the main components of an international logistics network. The three areas studied lead towards allowing students to give written and/or oral evidence to show that they can describe the operation of the component parts.

The three parts are:

- accurate description of inventory decisions in terms of the elements of the logistics network, where the inventory relates to stockholding costs, stock levels and push/pull systems

- accurate description of transport decisions in terms of the elements of the logistics network where the transport decisions relate to modal choice and combined transport

- accurate determination of warehouse facilities that are consistent with customer needs where the warehousing decisions relate to location and automation.

6.5 Answers to SAQs

SAQ 3.1

There are four types of stock, each of which has a value:

1. raw materials and components

2. work in progress (unfinished goods)

3. finished goods ready for sale

4. consumables, e.g. food and fuel.

SAQ 3.2

Health and safety aspects of stock control will be related to the type of stock. Issues such as how and where items are stored, how they are moved and who moves them might be significant. There may be hazardous materials on the premises, goods that deteriorate with time or items that are very heavy or awkward to move.

SAQ 3.4

The names of the alliances correspond to the web-site addresses. Information about each of them can be accessed at web-sites:

- *www.oneworldalliance.com*

- *www.skyteam.com*

- *www.star-alliance.com*

SAQ 3.5

There may be problems regarding job security, staffing, training or benefits. There are also issues about investment in the long term. Social considerations and safety/environmental issues must be addressed. Industry has separated and globalised.

During this process transport companies may have been concerned with linking markets on a global level. Now the transport industry is concerned with linking the complex production systems of transnational corporations.

These companies co-ordinate production, and design and manage facilities over many countries. To facilitate this they buy and invest in the capabilities of other countries. This is an example of foreign direct investment.

Environmental issues are now high on the list for consideration. The fossil fuel issue outlined in the Australian Petroleum Institute item highlights interesting issues.

SAQ 3.6

Inter-modal transport involves movement of goods in one loading unit or vehicle which uses successively a few methods of transport, without the goods themselves actually being handled.

Multimodal, or combined transportation involves transportation of goods by at least two means of transportation. The main reason for needing to know this distinction is that in the UK collection of transport statistics is mostly based on modal activity.

SAQ 3.7

(a)

- Grain

- Aggregates

- Coal

- Petroleum products (to distribution depots and large users)

- Chemicals (to depots and large users)

- Waste

- Cement.

Traffics using inland waterways may be inland, coastal (domestic), one-port (e.g. to offshore installations or for sea dredged aggregates), international or a combination of these categories.

(b)

Waterways are multifunctional. Well designed waterway track may provide opportunities for landscape enhancement, wildlife conservation, recreation, pedestrian access, land drainage, flood protection, water transfer and hydropower generation, some of which may contribute towards offsetting or sharing the costs involved.

Water transport uses less fuel, which means less pollution.

The greater fuel economy of waterborne freight transport means scarce resources are conserved and pollution is reduced because of low emissions. Water transport is quiet.

SAQ 3.8

Warehouses are more than just places to store goods.

They are an essential part of the operation of the supply chain. Inventory/stock levels kept in the warehouse, in current logistics services, are well managed for efficiency using electronic means.

6.6 Answers to activities

Activity 3.1

Minimum stock level — a minimum stock level is identified and re-order happens when that level is reached.

Stock review — regular reviews of stock when orders are placed to return stocks to a pre-determined level.

Just in time — aims to reduce costs by cutting stock to a minimum when they are ordered and used immediately.

Re-order lead time — allows for the time between placing an order and receiving it.

Economic order quantity — complex formula used to arrive at a balance between holding too little or too much stock.

Batch control — managing production in batches and ensuring that there are enough components to last till the next batch.

First in, first out — a system to ensure that perishable stock is used efficiently so that it does not deteriorate.

Activity 3.2

The transport issue will be of great importance to any warehouse owner in making a decision about where to locate. Different facilities will have different transport needs. There will be other considerations: the characteristics of the firm, business type, labour supply, space, potential growth, impact of technology, etc.

Locating a warehouse is a complex issue. The main factors to be considered when deciding on location include:

- costs and supply of labour

- market demand

- links to international markets

- infrastructures

- company growth

- technological development

- distribution questions.

Anyone deciding on the best location for warehousing

will take the decisions by considering all (or the current most important) of the factors relevant at four different levels. Different factors will be important at different stages:

Global decisions will be made by looking at the most important factors, such as market size, growth potential and the organisation's world-wide strategy. The really large companies will make these decisions on a day-to-day basis but, increasingly, smaller companies must be aware of the significance of such decisions.

National level decisions (choice of country) will still focus on market size and growth potential but other issues such as labour supply and the level of government support will be important. The legislation affecting logistics organisations will also have some bearing on final decisions.

Regional level decisions will be determined by access to wider networks, existing facilities and cost. It may also be a consideration that a business is located beside other, similar, organisations.

Local level decisions are mainly determined by space, accessibility and customers. Cost will also play a part.

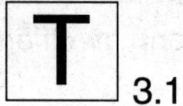

Tutor-marked assessment

Restricted-response questions:

- Describe inventory decisions in terms of the logistics network

- Describe transport decisions in terms of the logistics system

- Determine warehousing facilities which are consistent with customers needs.

Response to tutor-marked assessment

All points required for response are found in the text.

Make sure that all performance criteria are covered in your answer: stockholding costs, stock levels, push/pull systems, modal choice, combined transport, warehousing decisions, location, automation.

7

Section 4: Range of services provided

7.1 Introduction to this section

What this section is about

This section outlines the range of services provided by international logistics businesses, including logistics strategy and outsourcing/in-house provision as it is appropriate to the organisation.

Outcomes, aims and objectives

The aim is to provide evidence to demonstrate knowledge and/or skills by showing:

- correct description of the services provided by international logistics firms where the services are groupage and freight forwarding;

- explanation of the types of logistics services in terms of logistics strategy where the types are dedicated operators and shared user operators;

- comparison of in-house provision and outsourcing of logistics services appropriate to the organisation.

Approximate study time

12 hours.

Other resources required

Other resources required remain in line with those stated for the unit at the beginning of this study guide.

7.2 Assessment information for this section

How you will be assessed

Assessment will take the form of restricted-response questions.

When and where you will be assessed

Assessment will take place at a time and place decided by the providing centre.

What you have to achieve

Responses to the questions to include all performance criteria.

Opportunities for reassessment

Normally, you will be given one attempt to pass an assessment with one reassessment opportunity.

Your centre will also have a policy covering 'exceptional' circumstances, for example if you have been ill for an extended period of time. Each case will be considered on an individual basis and is at your centre's discretion (usually via written application), and they will decide whether or not to allow a third attempt. Please contact your tutor for details regarding how to apply.

7.3 Services provided by international logistics firms

Reliable freight transportation is the key to efficient distribution/supply chain networks. Whilst analysts, commentators and officials discuss bottlenecks, soaring freight rates and the need for more capacity in the infrastructure, managers are at work keeping the freight moving, getting it to its destination and preventing freight bills from going through the roof.

The industry is becoming ever more complex and time-sensitive. Managers must constantly respond to sophisticated demand and developments in, for example, information technology (IT), national/international legislation, emerging markets, new working practices and competitors' initiatives.

Many activities are performed within a company and every company within the logistics industry is in some way involved in supply chain relationships with other providers. In re-visiting the supply chain issue it is possible to identify the services provided by international logistics firms.

The structure of activities within and between companies is the key to creating good supply chain performance.

Successful supply chain management needs integration of business processes with other participants of the supply chain. When supply chains are not integrated valuable resources can be wasted.

The benefit of standardised business practice is that managers from different organisations in the supply chain can link their companies' operation with other members of the supply chain when necessary. The business processes are external and internal.

Implementation of supply chain management requires the formation of appropriate links with other members of the supply chain.

In an industry experiencing scarce resources, increased competition, higher customer expectation and faster rates of change, managers look towards partnership arrangements to strengthen the supply chain and provide for competitive advantage.

Sometimes partners can complement one another in terms of skills or expertise as well as business contacts.

The partnership approach allows for the enhancement of process and performance. It is a legal business arrangement and the actual outline of who does what will be included in the partnership agreement.

Self-Assessed Question

 4.1

What considerations should be taken into account when considering a partnership arrangement to provide the services offered by an international logistics firm?

Case study: Kelly International

Kelly International operates across a global network of 400 offices with around 20,000 logistics specialists. Worldwide, the company's comprehensive provision of products and services come together to provide integrated, value-creating supply chain solutions for its customers.

The company management attempt to meet companies' global business requirements in each of the local markets. Each part of the network has access to information which is required to maximise operation and service. There is an open and comprehensive information policy.

There are many aspects to the services offered by the company. Land freight and sea freight are an integral part of global trade. In partnerships with carriers, Kelly International is able to guarantee freight capacities and easily adapt to growing trade volumes — a key benefit when it comes to managing global supply chains.

The company continues to expand sea freight services to meet growing demands throughout its global network.

The company is also one of the world's leading providers of air freight services and comprehensive air logistics solutions. Annually, the company handles more than 350,000 tons of freight, serving the international key markets as well as offering individual transportation solutions to remote places.

Customers expect reliability in today's business community. That is why Kelly International air freight staff finds flexible solutions to meet customer needs around the globe. Consistent high levels of service and quality worldwide are ensured through a carefully selected choice of carriers, as well as good IT and operations systems, highly skilled staff, and individual planning and monitoring of each single shipment.

Kelly International is one of the leading contract logistics providers worldwide with 4.75 million square metres of warehouse and logistics space under its management across 35 countries.

The company wants to be known as partner of choice for logistics outsourcing and management of complex supply chain projects. Services offered cover all aspects of logistics planning, control and execution, from point of origin to consumption.

Contract logistics experts work closely both with the customer and all parts of company operation to maintain cost-effectiveness and service level requirements. There is continuous investment in new technologies to provide the best solutions and business intelligence.

The company, in line with many other logistics companies, continues to expand in global markets. This means that it has become more and more difficult to manage an increasing number of logistics partners and multiple contracts along with the complexity it brings to their supply chains. The company recognises this and has invested in good management to support its aim of being a lead logistics solutions provider.

The company aims to maintain highest standards in the areas of quality, safety and health, environment and security.

Self-Assessed Question

 4.2

1. What are the main services provided by Kelly International?

2. What other services would you expect an international logistics firm to provide?

Groupage services are often provided through specialist divisions of companies. They give customers the best level of service with accurate documentation and commitment to ensuring that the best possible rates are given to all. This applies regardless of whether customers require large commercial freight orders or one-off orders.

Many companies offering good groupage service pride themselves in giving customers individual service, tailor-made to their needs.

The actual groupage services provided include:

- door-to-door freight forwarding

- customised documentation

- customs brokerage

- export consolidation

- import services

- insurance facilities

- computerised order tracking.

Freight forwarding

Companies offering freight-forwarding services

assemble a portfolio of services that they can offer to potential clients. Normally the services can be offered individually or as part of a package of two or three services at one time.

Often air, ocean, rail and road freight forwarding services are offered to help companies find supply chain solutions. Freight-forwarding companies will generally provide access to global networks, comprehensive services and advanced IT systems. To help companies they will also manage transportation details such as shipment booking, carrier routing, tariffs and customs requirements. This saves precious time and resources that can be put to other uses.

Types of logistics services in terms of strategy

In international logistics there are many companies but few who offer a totally integrated service worldwide. This integrated approach offers quality, quick service incorporating road, rail and air freight services.

Companies who have this global capacity employ millions of people worldwide. In competitive markets these companies expand by a process of continuous acquisition, investment and diversification, and they hold contracts with major multinationals.

The large companies now operate in areas where

previously there were hundreds of smaller companies. They try to answer the client's every transport and logistical need. In so doing they sub-contract much of their work so there are still small firms in the industry but, increasingly, their work is determined by large companies.

The following article 'On the Move' was published in *Transport International*, issue no 21, October 2005. It provides a brief overview of the dominant companies and some of the projections for future growth.

7.4 On the move

They are huge, growing and operating in many transport sectors in virtually every country of the world. But who are the integrators and what do unions need to know about them?

Four companies dominate the thriving world of integrated express transport, in which road, rail and air freight services, which were once carried out by a plethora of local and national operations, are now controlled by giant global companies.

The big four — DHL, Federal Express, TNT, UPS — along with their many subcontractors employ well over a million people worldwide. Thousands more are employed by other smaller, but growing companies.

By 2008 the 'integrators' are expected to be pulling in around US$42.4 billion between them — an increase of

20 per cent since 2003*. In this intensely competitive market the big companies are expanding through a continual process of acquisition, investment and diversification into newer areas such as supply chain management. All hold contracts with major multinational companies, including Samsung, Toyota, BMW, Nestle, Colgate-Palmolive and Canon* to name a few, and set out to answer their clients' every transport and logistical need.

While each of the big four companies is currently strongest in its home region, all are fighting for new business in other regions. Asia Pacific (and particularly China) is the key market but they are also expanding into Central and South American markets.

The impact of constant movement and reorganisation in integrated transport is felt by thousands of workers in many different ways. When companies change hands, jobs are affected. Often a local or national workforce finds itself swallowed up into a vast global machine, under the control of a far distant employer. A union membership base may be split when the new employer begins to subcontract out company services.

The companies involved have varying relationships with trade unions, though union density — with the notable exceptions of UPS in the USA and DHL in Germany — is generally low. Some unions have reported a good relationship. Others have started with hostility which has then improved. But in some cases the company is anti-union all the time.

Human resources issues appear in most cases to be directed centrally from the headquarters or regional office and not locally. In theory at least, this means there should be corporate-wide policies relating to labour conditions and trade union recognition.

A policy-making centre provides a clear target to unions when engaging in international cooperation and solidarity with their counterparts overseas. The apparent sensitivity of these companies about their public image presents another opportunity for the unions, while the highly time-sensitive nature of the operations of the integrators may present an aspect of vulnerability to industrial pressure.

Coordinating labour responses

For the first time, ITF affiliates from 16 countries attended an international meeting of integrators in London in February 2005 in order to find ways of using international union coordination as a tool to assist their organising efforts in the integrator companies. The ITF also works on this issue in cooperation with the global union federation UNI, which organises postal workers around the world.

Sharing their experiences of the companies operating in their countries, unions agreed to set up a network, coordinated by the ITF, and to work together on developing a set of minimum labour standards for adoption throughout the industry.

One possibility is that these standards could be reflected in an International Framework Agreement to be developed between ITF unions and integrator companies. In this case, a coordinated process of international collective bargaining would help to ensure implementation of the agreement in the different companies.

Through taking part in a process of cooperation, delegates to the meeting in London expressed the hope they would be able to motivate members in their own countries to support a dispute that may be taking place in the same company, but hundreds or thousands of miles away. They hoped to utilise this year's ITF Road Transport Action Week Campaign on 10 – 16 October to promote initial demands.

Network members are also expected to meet in November in Washington DC at the invitation of the Teamsters union (IBT). Meanwhile the ITF is writing to top management of the companies asking for clarification of their corporate policies relating to industrial relations. From union reports to date, it appears that irrespective of central policies, the integrators tend to tailor their industrial relations approach to exploit circumstances in their different countries or regions of operation.

*Data taken from the Initial Report on DHL, UPS, FedEx and TNT, by Paula Hamilton, ITF/University of London logistics project worker.

Profiles

TNT

Thomas Nationwide Transport was founded in Australia in 1946, and initially focused on express delivery services only. The parent company TNT NV now incorporates two main brands: TNT (express and logistics services) and Royal TPG Post, the national postal operator in the Netherlands, which also operates in Europe and worldwide. The group employs over 160,000 people in 63 countries.

The company claims TNT Express has the biggest integrated express air and road network in Europe, while TNT Logistics is the second biggest logistics company in the world.

TNT has declared its adoption and support for the 10 principles of the United Nations Global Compact (www.unglobalcompact.org) with respect to human rights, labour (including union) rights and the protection of the environment.

FedEx

Federal Express was launched as an express transportation service in the USA in 1973 and began expanding into the Asia Pacific region in the early 1980s. It acquired flying rights to 21 Asian countries and regions in 1989 through its purchase of the all-cargo airline, the Flying Tigers.

It now employs over 138,000 staff and serves 378 airports worldwide.

The company claims to be the world's largest express transportation company, transporting more than 3.2 million items in 220 countries per day. FedEx has more than 138,000 employees, 50,000 drop-off locations, 671 aircraft and 41,000 vehicles in its integrated global network.

Like all the other big integrators, the company has invested a great deal in IT. It has diversified its services to the extent of offering colour printing, Internet access, videoconferencing and other services.

FedEx is widely considered to be anti-union and has the lowest union density of any of the big four integrators.

DHL

Since 2002 DHL has been wholly owned by Deutsche Post World Net, Europe's biggest postal service provider, which consolidated all its express and logistics companies — including Deutsche Post Euro Express and Danzas — into the DHL brand in 2003.

The company was founded in San Francisco in 1969 when the founders Adrian Dalsey, Larry Hillblom and Robert Lynn began personally transporting papers by air. This allowed them to begin customs clearance of ships' cargo ahead of the ships' arrival, thereby reducing waiting time in the harbour. The company claims in this way to have been the founder of the international air express business.

By 1979 it was transporting not only papers but also packages. In 1988 DHL was present in 170 countries and employed 16,000 staff. Today it employs almost 350,000 staff and, on top of its express package delivery service, provides, road, rail, air and ocean freight transport as well as warehousing, distribution, supply chain management and other logistics solutions.

DHL has a variable relationship with the unions, but in several countries, including the US and India, the relationship can be described as poor.

The company tactic of widespread sub-contracting

allows it to sidestep many employee and trade union regulations and keep costs down, simply ending contracts and moving on when pressures mount for pay rises or union representation.

At the same time the company achieves a consistent corporate image by insisting that subcontractors take on its yellow and red livery.

UPS

Founded in 1907 as a messenger company in the USA, UPS now employs 40,000 workers outside the USA as well as 317,000 in its home country. It gives emphasis to the goal of 'enabling commerce around the globe'. The company claims it is the world's largest package delivery company as well as being a global logistics provider.

The company has been recognised as a 'good employer' in a number of corporate and ethical awards. A commitment to recognising and negotiating fairly with trade unions is enshrined in UPS's company-wide 'policy book' and it appears to maintain a generally positive relationship with the unions. However, relations with the Teamsters have not fully recovered from a major dispute in 1997, which showed the potential of international campaigning for building on union power.

As well as strong rank and file support in the USA, the

strike gained international backing from the ITF and a strong campaign following in Europe, UPS's most important market outside of North America. UPS ended the strike by conceding a favourable contract before simultaneous walkouts to be staged by unions in Belgium, Holland, France and Germany went ahead.

(Source: *Transport International* 21 October 2005; http://www.itfglobal.org/transport-international/ti21onmove.cfm)

International Logistics
Unit Student Guide

China Modern Economic Publishing House

Self-Assessed Question

 4.3 Outline the labour issues identified in the above article.

7.5 In-house provision and outsourcing

Only the larger firms can realistically expect to offer all of the services grouped under logistics. Smaller companies will continue to offer in-house services for the specialist niche areas in which they operate, but increasingly will outsource specialist work to other companies.

It would be unlikely, for example, that a very small transport company would have the internal expertise, or the financing, to keep pace with electronic systems software developed specifically for the logistics industry.

They would outsource this work to companies specialising in that area of work. The same could be said where small companies are trying to keep pace with legislative change.

7.6 Outsourcing logistics services

As stated, the large companies outsource much of their work. This may involve outsourcing to independent companies or to internal divisions.

By outsourcing to a logistics outsourcing specialist it is possible to store and distribute products efficiently whilst decreasing costs, maximising resources and satisfying customers.

Companies can concentrate on core competencies. That means doing what they do well and looking at what the companies they wish to outsource to and deciding what they do better.

Moving from in-house management to a third party logistics provider may result in the following advantages:

- reduced time in reaching desired market

- good customer satisfaction and retention

- warehouse management solutions

- more time and money to spend on core activities

- reduced staff and operating costs.

Experienced outsourcers continuously develop and refine the best ways in which they can deal with the companies they work with. Sometimes they find it beneficial to work in partnership with the outsource company. Outsourcing is definitely a business relationship.

Outsourcing is more than a cost-saving mechanism. Smart decision-makers know that outsourcing is an indispensable business tool to not only reduce cost, but to drive business value into their enterprises.

The International Association of Outsourcing Professionals (IAOP) helps member businesses access the best outsourcing opportunities worldwide.

As business has gone global, companies have come to realise that the need to find reliable business outsource partners is a necessity. Organisations like the IAOP help them keep pace with new ideas and new ways of doing business worldwide.

Customers of logistics services are seeking greater reliability at consistently lower cost at local, sub-continent and global levels.

As higher performance from better end-to-end integration (better e-commerce, etc.) becomes possible, approaches made by different operators will become divergent.

Customers recognise the full value of trade-offs from outsourcing and the logistics providers are driven by customer needs.

One useful approach to looking at the outsourcing issue may be to pose questions about why a company would outsource in certain situations:

Why outsource air freight?

There may not be real choices here, especially for smaller companies. Goods which are to be transported across the globe need to be moved quickly and the best way of doing this is to send them by air.

It may be possible, but not best policy, to deal with multiple carriers, but to meet deadlines it will be easier to deal with a global air freight provider operating in the main business centres worldwide.

Many companies specialise in offering a single source to manage global air freight, offering a range of services to meet shipping needs.

Why outsource sea freight?

Specialist companies can handle almost any size of shipment. This covers part container loads, full container loads, oversized cargos and specialised cargos.

Their dedicated, advanced tracking systems can follow cargo progress. Such companies can operate from most points of origin, arrange pick-up and delivery and manage shipping documentation.

The benefits are that shipping is simplified and solutions concerning volume, timing and pricing can be easily found.

Why outsource rail or road freight?

Rail is a cost-effective way of shipping goods, as is

road transport. Maintaining transport in this area is a huge cost and is often best provided by carriers specialising in the appropriate mode.

Why outsource specialised freight?

Special loads often have to be transported on specially modified transport. Often they require to be managed by people who have detailed knowledge of environmental and safety legislation.

The shipments may be sensitive and/or high value, meaning that there is a high insurance cost and perhaps constraints imposed on how transportation should take place.

Why outsource time-sensitive freight?

To get it to the destination intact and at the stated time. Specialist companies can manage this process.

Self-Assessed Question

 4.4

Outsourcing certainly appears to cut costs by providing for the lowest cost per unit method of transporting goods. Apart from unit costs what other costs should be considered?

7.7 Location of companies

Manufacturing industries are dependant on logistics services. The secondary stage in production takes the raw materials and turns them into goods which have to be taken to the location where demand for them is to be satisfied.

Who, what, where and how are questions which are constants in the industry. When a company is considering setting up a new manufacturing industry or looking at ways of maximising use of current resources the questions become serious.

Successful product development is a key issue in the success of manufacturing organisations. Other considerations are also of prime importance to the future business success. They include *strategic site planning*, which includes facilities, layout and potential expansion. The actual site of an operation is the first step to successful manufacturing. Questions about labour sources and whether there is an adequate transport infrastructure are also crucial.

7.8 Representation for freight forwarders

The International Federation of Freight Forwarders Associations (FIATA) is a non-governmental organisation covering approximately 40,000 forwarding and logistics firms.

It has consultative status with the Economics and Social Council (ECOSOC) of the United Nations, the United Nations Conference on Trade and Development

(UNCTAD) and the UN Commission on International Trade Law (UNCITRAL).

It is recognised as representing the freight-forwarding industry by the International Chamber of Commerce (ICC), the International Air Transport Association (IATA), the International Union of Railways (UIC), the International Road Transport Union (IRU), the World Customs Organisation (WCO) and the World Trade Organisation (WTO). FIATA is the largest non-governmental organisation in the field of transportation. It has worldwide influence.

7.9 Marketing plans

As part of the overall business plan for any organisation the marketing section explains how it is planned to get customers to buy goods and/or services. The marketing plan includes sections detailing the:

- products and/or services and your unique selling proposition

- pricing strategy

- sales/distribution plan

- advertising and promotions plan.

The easiest way to develop your marketing plan is to work through each of these sections, referring to the market research you completed when you were writing the previous sections of the business plan.

(Note that if you are developing a marketing plan on its own, rather than as part of a business plan, the marketing plan will also need to include a target market and a competitive analysis section).

Regardless of whether a company within the logistics industry is outsourcing or keeping an operation in-house there will have to be reference to a business plan.

The main focus for this section, relating to such a plan, is to do with distribution plans. It is important to know that these plans are not done in isolation from the overall business goals.

Remember, the primary goal of the marketing plan is to get people to buy your products or services. The sales and distribution part of the marketing plan details how this is going to happen.

Traditionally there are three parts to the sales and distribution section of the marketing plan, although all three parts may not apply to your business.

1. Outline the distribution methods to be used

How is your product or service going to get to the customer? For instance, will you distribute your product or service through a website, through the mail, through sales representatives, or through retail?

What distribution channel is going to be used? In a direct distribution channel, the product or service goes directly from the manufacturer to the consumer. In a one-stage distribution channel it goes from manufacturer to retailer to consumer. The traditional distribution channel is from manufacturer to wholesaler to retailer to consumer. Outline all the different companies, people and/or technologies that will be involved in the process of getting your product or service to your customer.

- What are the costs associated with distribution?

- What are the delivery terms?

- How will the distribution methods affect production time frames or delivery? (How long will it take to get your product or service to your customer?)

If your business involves selling a product, you should also include information about inventory levels and packaging in this part of your marketing plan. For instance:

- How are your products to be packaged for shipping and for display?

- Does the packaging meet all regulatory requirements

(such as labelling)?

- Is the packaging appropriately coded, priced and complementary to the product?

- What minimum inventory levels must be maintained to ensure that there is no loss of sales due to problems such as late shipments and back orders?

2. Outline the transaction process between your business and your customers

- What system will be used for processing orders, shipping and billing?

- What methods of payment will customers be able to use?

- What credit terms will customers be offered? If you will offer discounts for early payment or impose penalties for late payment, they should be mentioned in this part of your marketing plan.

- What is your return policy?

- What warranties will the customer be offered? Describe these or any other services.

- What after-sales support will you offer customers and what will you charge (if anything) for this support?

- Is there a system for customer feedback so customer satisfaction (or the lack of it) can be tracked and addressed?

3. If it is applicable to your business, outline your sales strategy

What types of salespeople will be involved (commissioned salespeople, product demonstrators, telephone solicitors, etc.)?

Describe your expectations of these salespeople and how sales effectiveness will be measured.

Will a sales training programme be offered? If so, describe it in this section of the marketing plan.

Describe the incentives salespeople will be offered to encourage their achievements (such as getting new accounts, the most orders, etc.).

Lastly, when you are writing a marketing plan, you need to develop an advertising and promotion plan.

7.10 Summary of this section

This section concentrates on looking at the range of services provided by international logistics companies. There is a return to the outline of supply chain management and partnership working in order to look at the benefits for individual companies of providing services within a framework that maximises performance.

The services offered are identified and concentration applied to groupage and freight forwarding.

Explanation is provided for type of logistics services in terms of logistics strategy for dedicated operators and shared user operators.

Comparison is provided for in-house provision and outsourcing of logistics services appropriate to an organisation.

Tutor-marked assignment

1. Describe the services offered by international logistics firms. Use examples to illustrate your answer.

2. Explain logistics services in terms of strategy. Use examples to illustrate your answer.

3. Compare in-house and outsourcing of logistics. Use examples to illustrate your answer.

The points required for completion of this assessment are included in the text.

7.11 Answers to SAQs

SAQ 4.1

Partnerships are costly in monetary, time and effort terms. It is, therefore, impossible to form a partnership with every supplier, customer or third-party provider. Scarce resources should only be used to link with organisations where partnership working really benefits both.

All partnerships are not the same. Partnership working offers a systematic process for developing, implementing and improving corporate relationships. It can provide a route to effective and efficient business relationships in an industry looking for competitive advantage.

They require to conform to a legal set-up.

SAQ 4.2

1. The company provides road air and sea freight services. It also provides information for customers and offers logistics solutions.

2. Other services could include solutions for carriage of consumer goods, consumables, retail and online companies. There could be warehousing solutions, outsourcing, specialist delivery opportunities and

many more.

SAQ 4.3

The impact of constant movement and reorganisation in integrated transport is felt by thousands of workers in many different ways. When companies change hands, jobs are affected.

Often a local or national workforce finds itself swallowed up into a vast global machine under the control of a far distant employer. A union membership base may be split when the new employer begins to subcontract out company services.

Human resources issues appear in most cases to be directed centrally from the headquarters or regional office and not locally. In theory at least this means there should be corporate-wide policies relating to labour conditions and trade union recognition.

SAQ 4.4

Other costs may include customs and duties, banking fees, insurance and costs relating to any delays.

8 Section 5: Forces of change and future developments

8.1 Introduction to this section

What this section is about

This section is about the forces of change impacting on the future development of international logistics.

Outcomes, aims and objectives

The aim is to identify issues which are having huge impact on the way carriers operate and look at some of the points to be considered in future planning.

Approximate study time

12 hours.

Other resources required

The resources required are as those mentioned at the beginning of this guide and in each of the previous four outcomes.

8.2 Assessment information for this section

How you will be assessed

Assessment will be by means of restricted-response questions. Centres may provide alternative assessment as mentioned at the beginning of this guide.

When and where you will be assessed

Assessment will take place at the discretion of the centre.

What you have to achieve

Satisfactory completion of the questions incorporating all points in the performance criteria.

Opportunities for reassessment

Normally, you will be given one attempt to pass an assessment with one reassessment opportunity.

Your centre will also have a policy covering 'exceptional' circumstances, for example if you have been ill for an extended period of time. Each case will be considered on an individual basis and is at your centre's discretion (usually via written application), and they will decide whether or not to allow a third attempt. Please contact your tutor for details regarding how to apply.

8.3 Change impacting on the future development of international logistics

There are three main areas for potential future change in the logistics industry featured in this section:

1. electronic data interchange

2. reverse logistics

3. green logistics.

8.4 Electronic data interchange

Information must flow between internal and external customers. Investment in technology is crucial to all parts of the industry for corporate effectiveness.

Good systems are required at all levels as logistics as a process interacts with many sections within and outside a company.

The systems must be robust in order to handle/process orders, plan production, source materials and distribute goods/services. Some of the challenges facing the industry include:

- Response time — In a global marketplace it is necessary to respond very quickly to any change. There may be changes to the company forecasts, customer requirements and response to new products by competitors. The crucial factor is that all such changes must be managed⋯quickly!!

- Service — As discussed in Section 2, good customer service is essential

- Costs — There is a very difficult balance to be maintained when setting costs. The cost cannot be set in isolation from the overall service provision. Costs include transportation costs, labour costs, warehousing costs, marketing costs, etc. Often forgotten, but also contributing to costs, is the possibility of fluctuation on world currency markets. The movement of goods worldwide necessitates transactions in many currencies. It is also the case that these currencies will constantly fluctuate, sometimes requiring intervention in cargo shipment.

There are many challenges for the industry. In discussion of the growth in requirements for technology and need to respond to environmental issues it is worth pausing to consider again what we mean by logistics. In so doing the main requirements in response to change will become a bit clearer.

Logistics is a process. The spectrum of activity reaches from the seller to the customer. It interacts with all provision within the company and with many organisations outside the company.

Change is constant. The challenge is to keep up with change and still maintain profitability within increasingly strict environmental guidelines.

Electronic data interchange (EDI) is used for the automated transfer and exchange of documents between diverse operations/applications.

This technology is used extensively and allows all partners in a supply chain to exchange invoices, purchase orders, information requests and other important business documents from one business system to another.

There is no need for human intervention if this type of system is operating so there are obvious advantages for all partners.

There are fewer errors, faster responses, lower administrative costs and a good system will be easy to use, reliable and versatile. EDI systems incorporate secure file transfer systems that move data from one application to another and protect it from harm in transit.

This level of integration allows for transfers between private channels or the Internet without possibility of interception or alteration.

Self-Assessed Question

5.1

From your knowledge of information requirements of organisations, list documents that could be exchanged by means of electronic data interchange.

Self-Assessed Question

 5.2

How would you define electronic data interchange?

The most basic advantage of using an EDI system is that it cuts out the need for repetition of manual tasks. Use of agreed product codes, location codes and prices eliminates the need for re-keying of information and delivers robust data.

EDI enables suppliers to minimise costs, provide good customer care and provide reliable information for partners.

In practice, EDI is widely used in many sectors, including catering, grocery, department stores and publishing. However, there are no barriers to its use across most industry sectors and it may benefit partners in electronics and government intelligence.

The most common application is the automated sale and purchase of goods and services. It is surprising that this system (in spite of huge number of transactions) is not as widely known about as, for example, the Internet.

In the logistics industry network-based transportation solutions support the business requirements of a wide range of companies from the smallest local carrier to some of the largest organisations in the world.

It is necessary to have 'smart' solutions for ever-challenging customer requirements. The needs of the transportation industry ultimately require integration of distribution systems. EDI-based carriers send out and receive data and can also use the web as back-up.

It is also possible to have a carbon copy system by which means a file can be sent to multiple receivers. There can be a customised service for each receiver. EDI can also support scheduled transmissions, event-driven transmissions and real-time transmissions.

There are many data formats used within an EDI system.

The arguments for and against use of EDI

All interchange systems have their advantages and disadvantages. The main ones for EDI are as follows.

Advantages

- Time savings

- Elimination of need for multiple hard copies of documentation

- Easy access to data

- Improved inter-departmental/inter-industry communication

- Efficient tracking of information

- Cost savings

- Accuracy of information

- Non-time-based transfer of information.

Disadvantages

- Change is always difficult

- Original paper system may not be suited to EDI

- Initial setup costs may be high.

EDI involves the use of secure private networks known as value-added networks (VANs). These networks provide specialised services to assist reliable and secure delivery of information between communicators.

VANs are accessed by means of specialist communications software. The software provides access to a mailbox. The EDI system is often PC based.

Some of the main global companies offering value added networks are IBM, BT and GXS.

As mentioned, EDIs are computer based. In the past few years there has been a move towards the use of AS2 (Applicability Statement 2), a system using the Internet to provide real-time message delivery without the need to have VANs. AS2 is a specification regarding how data can be transported. This statement specifies how to connect, deliver, validate and acknowledge data.

The implementation of this standard requires two machines, i.e. a client and a server, communicating, one with the other, over the Internet. Usually, on receipt of a message the receiver sends an acknowledgement called a message disposition notification (MDN) back to the server.

Activity

5.1

Using the Internet to access some of the companies providing AS2 help, find out the following (you may wish to start with sites like www.axway.com, www.porthus.com):

1. What are the advantages of its use?

2. What are the disadvantages of its use?

3. Are there other protocols for transferring information over the Internet?

4. Why is exchanging data securely important?

Self-Assessed Question

 5.3

Why is it so important to design systems to exchange data securely?

EDI standards

There are standards to be adhered to when using EDI systems.

As mentioned, EDI is exchange of structured information from one computer to another electronically with a minimum of human input. This requires standardisation of the methods used.

Specific interchange methods are agreed on by standards bodies (national and international).

From their design stage EDI standards were separate and independent from lower level technology. They allow for transmission using Internet protocols and private networks.

EDI documents contain the same type of information as found in paper documents.

An example of this is EDI940. This standard is the equivalent of paper documentation requesting movement of goods to a retailer from a warehouse. In trying to visualise the format of standards they can be seen like a spreadsheet where every cell formats part of the message.

The standards state the ways in which information

must be used. Examples will be what information is essential/optional for a document and how the actual document is to be structured.

There are two main sets of EDI standards: UN/EDIFACT and XML.

UN/EDIFACT

The United Nations Directories for Electronic Interchange of Administration, Commerce and Transport are briefly explained (below). They are available to download at: www.unece.org/trade.

EDI for administration, commerce and transport

United Nations rules for EDI for Administration, Commerce and Transport comprise a set of internationally agreed-upon standards, directories and guidelines for the electronic interchange of structured data related to trade in goods and services between independent computerised information systems.

This standard, referred to as UN/EDIFACT, has been taken on board by the International Organisation for Standardisation (ISO) and is ISO 9735. This standard is continuously monitored and developed by the United Nations Centre for Trade Facilitation and Electronic Business (UN/CEFACT). EDIFACT standardisation provides for:

- standard messages (between all industries/countries)

- interactive exchange protocol

- a set of syntax rules to structure data.

EDIFACT standards are widely used in the tourism and civil aviation industries. Adopted early on by European institutions this standard is likely to be adhered to for some time to come because of the cost involved in changing software. The original standards used in the UK, TRADACOMS, are being replaced by EDIFACT standards. In the USA ANSI X 12 is widely used but is also being replaced by EDIFACT.

XML

It is important to point out that it is likely that UK and US companies will have to support/integrate more that one standard into their EDI operations. Global enterprise is what it is all about so data must reach the right people at the right time and in the right format.

Asian regions adopted standards later than their European partners and because of this tend to have implemented B2B systems using XML (extensible mark-up language) standards. The XML languages (there are many languages based on XML, e.g. RSS XHTML) allow for sharing of data across different information systems.

Fundamentally, all information in the XML system is text based with 'mark-ups' indicating where information is separated into appropriate fields.

The main benefits of using XML are:

- it is in a format that can be read by people and machines at the same time

- most information in written languages can be communicated

- it is based on international standards

- it can be used for document storage.

It is suitable for most (not all) types of documents There are some problems with using XML:

- there are problems with complex syntax

- it may only be useful for storage only if the file is of low volume.

The standards for EDI were meant to be independent of data transmitted using Internet protocols and private networks (sometimes referred to as lower level technologies).

There is a need to differentiate between the actual EDI documents and the methods used for transmitting them. This is a growth area with potential for the development of many sub-sets from the main standardised systems.

The specifications do not always make clear how data should be interpreted, e.g. in making a statement about quantity ordered. Clarity is required as to exactly what is meant by a 'box', 'carton', etc.

An EDI document ordering a factory manager to send out a load is an *inbound document* in relation to the factory computer system. It is an *outbound document* in relation to the person that transmitted the document.

Inbound and outbound refers to the direction of the transmission. EDI translation software offers the interface between an internal system and the standards adhered to. The translation mechanism is not part of the standard.

Before leaving discussion of EDI it is worth re-visiting the issue of voice synthesisation mentioned in connection to warehousing in Section 3.

This is another use of technology that is having a significant impact on the way parts of the supply chain operate. Data interpretation is this example is hugely successful in terms of accuracy.

The most common application is order picking, where improved accuracy and productivity offer fast results.

Companies wishing to use this technology can use existing radio frequency networks as long as they have compliant access points. Reports indicate that order picking results show 99.9% accuracy (manual picking errors may be between 80 and 90%).

Another bonus side effect of using this type of technology is that there are fewer safety issues as hands and eyes are freed up. The system can even be used in freezers, down to a temperature of $-29°C$ and in noisy warehouse and distribution depots.

Speech recognition technology can accurately recognise individual speakers regardless of accent or dialect. Normally each user will have their individual belts and headsets, and the voice will be downloaded to terminal within seconds. It is easy to imagine the benefits of this technology in large warehouses, container ports, air terminals, transport hubs and distribution depots.

8.5 Reverse logistics

'Taking things back' may be the easiest way to describe what happens in a reverse logistics situation. Issues for the producers are discussed later in the section after an outline of some of the reasons for the need for reverse logistics.

The manufacturer of a product may issue a request to return items, usually because there are safety reasons.

Recall can be for a small sample batch or a full-scale production run. They also require that goods are returned from a customer or wholesaler to the original producer; this involves a huge amount of work for those involved in the logistics industry.

Recalls are done to limit potential harm to users. Usually the recall also:

- limits possibility of company being sued for corporate negligence

- limits bad publicity for the company.

Recalls are costly for the company because they may involve payment for damages. At one point Toyota car manufacturers recalled 500,000 Toyota Tundra pickup trucks because of steering problems which had resulted in several accidents. The cost of this would have been high.

Each country has laws for protection of consumers and therefore a product may be recalled from one country and not from another (specific requirements will vary). In some countries consumer laws may include regulations stating how much of the cost the maker will have to bear, situations in which recall is compulsory and penalties to be imposed for failure to recall.

Generally producers will recall voluntarily but on

occasions the recall is enforced under the consumer legislation in the country and penalties will apply, as appropriate.

For the company recalls are, as stated above, usually very costly as there will be the need to replace and respond to any legal action. In some cases the companies will not publicise the recall, in which case the general public has to depend on consumer groups or government agencies to raise awareness.

There are several steps taken in most situations in which there is a product recall (minor variations will depend on the legislation in countries where the recall is taking place). The stages are:

- The manufacturer tells authorities which product(s) they intend to recall, including batch numbers serial numbers

- Announcements are made on government websites and specific newspapers

- Consumers groups may use a variety of outlets to inform consumers

- Advice given to consumers usually involves returning item to receive modification or refund

- Compensation issues are explored.

The following example illustrates how product recall is publicised on UK government websites. The Food Standards Agency (www.food.gov.uk) posts all such notices relating to food products.

Cow & Gate product recall

Wednesday 09 February 2005

Cow & Gate Ltd has recalled a batch of its Cheese and Tomato Bake packet meal because it is labelled incorrectly as being milk and lactose-free. The Agency has issued a Food Alert For Information.

Product details

Cow & Gate Cheese and Tomato Bake Packet Meal from 4 months (125 g) new improved recipe

Best Before: 18/02/06, 10/03/06, 11/03/06, 05/04/06.

Although it can be safely eaten by most babies, because of the incorrect claim it is unsuitable for infants who are allergic or intolerant to cows' milk and dairy products.

No other batches/date codes, or any other Cow & Gate products are known to be affected.

The company has issued a product recall, which will

appear in national newspapers on 10 and 11 February 2005. It has also set up a helpline on 0800 0830252.

Point of sale notices will also be placed in Boots, Asda and Tesco stores.

If your baby has an allergy or intolerance to cows' milk and dairy products and you have some of the affected product, you should throw the product away.

For a full refund you can you return the base of the pack showing the best before date, together with your name and address, to:

Consumer Assurance

Cow & Gate

Newmarket Avenue

White Horse Business Park

Trowbridge

Wiltshire

BA14 0XQ

Activity

5.2

Consider some well-known companies who have made worldwide product recalls (or companies in your country who have made recalls).

In the UK government agencies offer help to companies recalling products.

A good example is to be found from Trading Standards, who offer the facility to post company information on their website. This short list below illustrates the number of recalls happening over a very short period of time (those that are publicised).

Some recent postings are listed below.

Product safety recalls

If you would like your Product Recall or Safety Notice to appear on this site email it to publications@tsi.org.uk

- 01/02/07 — IKEA PARODI and APELSIN Glass Vases — Recalls

- 18/01/07 — TJ Hughes Children's Teddy Bear Snowsuits and Jackets — Recall

- 15/01/07 — Lloydspharmacy Little Angels Party Bubble Machine — Recall

- 12/01/07 — Set of 6 Chocolate Candles — Recall

- 11/01/07 — WHSmith Children's Dough Sets — Recall

- 11/01/07 — Marks & Spencer Light-Up Rattle — Recall

- 11/01/07 — Marks & Spencer Glass & Stainless Steel Kettle — Recall

- 29/12/06 — Safety Notice: Míele Revolution Vacuum Cleaners

- 22/12/06 — NEXT Little Angel and Rodney Baking Kit — Recall

- 22/12/06 — Tesco Indoor Christmas Lights — Recall

- 21/12/06 — Moving Picture First Mountain — Recall

- 19/12/06 — Findus Gourmet 6 Salmon Skewers 360g — Recall

- 15/12/06 — ASDA and Birds Eye Branded Frozen Ready Meals — Recall

- 15/12/06 — Safety Notice: Viking RescYou Liferafts

- 14/12/06 — The First Years® Shake 'n Jingle Keys — Recall

- 14/12/06 — Sainsbury's Chicken Frozen Ready Meals — Recall

- 14/12/06 — Tesco's Own Brand Hot Salsa Dip 300g — Recall

- 11/12/06 — QS Baby Fur Trim Puffa Jacket — Recall

- 11/12/06 — Welkin Portable DVD Player Battery Pack — Recall

- 08/12/06 — Zippy Soft Toys — Recall

- 04/12/06 — Nature's Table Hawaiian Mix — Recall

- 30/11/06 — Matalan Lighting Chains — Recall

- 28/11/06 — ASDA Pre-Lit Christmas Trees — Recall

- 23/11/06 — Safety Notice: Bionaire 3kW Oil Filled Heater

- 22/11/06 — Safety Notice: England's Professional Lifejackets

- 22/11/06 — Heinz Toddler's Own Sweet Potato Beef Casserole — Recall

- 22/11/06 — Boots Delicious Caramel Shortcake — Recall

- 21/11/06 — Clarks Boys Snow Boot with Toggle — Recall

- 21/11/06 — Batchelors Super Noodles Chicken Flavour 100g — Recall

- 20/11/06 — George Taffeta Dress — Recall

- 20/11/06 — Safety Notice: JS Air Curtains SM Controller

- 17/11/06 — SPAR Flapjacks 90g — Recall

- 17/11/06 — Northern Catch 15 Seafood Sticks — Recall

- 17/11/06 — Sainsbury's Crisps — Recall

- 07/11/06 — Heinz Chicken & Mushroom Toast Toppers 128g — Recall

- 06/11/06 — NISA Today Heritage Garlic Sausage and Pork Luncheon Meat — Recall

- 06/11/06 — Waitrose Frozen Chicken Breast Chunks 300g — Recall

- 03/11/06 — Nairn's Organic Herb Oatcakes — Recall

- 03/11/06 — Waitrose Natural Cottage Cheese 500g — Recall

- 02/11/06 — ASDA Simply Porridge 500g — Recall

Source: www.tradingstandards.gov.uk

When problems are encountered with goods and services brought into the UK from other EU member states consumers can access 10 European Consumer Information Centres (Euroguichet), supported by the European Commission, which provide information and, sometimes, conciliation for cross-border disputes.

Similar organisations operate in other parts of the world.

In the USA recent recalls are listed at www.Recalls.gov.

Issues for the logistics industry (reverse logistics and recycling)

Product recall is one aspect of a process which involves taking products from a point in the supply chain. Other examples of situations which would qualify as being determined as **reverse logistics** are:

- out-of-date produce/merchandise

- returns from consumers

- redistribution of merchandise

- overstocked goods.

Reverse logistics can be simply defined as 'activities

involved in removing/redirecting a product or service after the original point of sale'. The overall aim is to maximise the value of the merchandise.

Reverse logistics planning will involve many different plans from forward logistics.

Good storage and packaging systems will be required to make sure that careful handling minimises any loss of product value. The returned goods may be kept in warehouses for storage, recycling, return to original manufactures for payment, selling in another market or combinations of all of these.

A good example of reverse logistics can often be seen at local outdoor markets. A stall may have been set up to 'get rid of' a large amount of ladies clothing.

Some of it may be branded. Most of the time the clothes will have some minor flaw — perhaps seams are not finished off or logos are not well printed. The flaws may not be obvious to the untrained eye but the goods are being sold to maximise returns ('perfects' would be sold at much higher prices but customers could return them as substandard).

'Seconds shops' generally sell inventory overloads or sub-standard goods. Others involved in reverse logistics may be active in warehousing, recycling, repair and waste re-usage.

Main problems with reverse logistics

1. Many companies do not realise that if the process is well managed it can create a competitive advantage for the organisation.

2. Some organisations believe that when merchandise is delivered their responsibility ends.

3. When there is no adequate link between internal and external administration systems reverse logistics often do not receive the same attention as forward logistics. Activities such as transportation, warehousing and inventory control are similar in most logistics operations, but sometimes they are not identical in forward and reverse activities.

4. Sufficient personnel, time and money must be dedicated to reverse logistics. This is not always the case.

5. In some companies returned goods are thought to be less important than at the point of original sale, resulting in the goods being in the logistics system for longer.

6. Firms are not always clear about when, what kinds of products and how many products are returned.

International Logistics
Unit Student Guide

Self-Assessed Question

 5.4

What can companies do to improve the process and highlight the importance of reverse logistics?

Recycling involves changing materials into new products. In doing this scarce materials are not wasted and the overall consumption of raw materials and energy is reduced. Recycling is often referred to as 'waste management'.

It does not simply involve re-use. It is a situation where a process results in a new format and use for materials.

Activity

5.3

Make a list of materials that may be recycled.

Linking logistics with disposal of waste material and recycling (including toxic and hazardous goods) has resulted in an extension of the market for logistics companies. Customer-driven domestic waste is set aside, involving the general public at local levels. Hazardous material is transported to designated sites and manufacturers take responsibility for delivery of new products as well as returns.

Customer-driven recycling comes from a customer-driven base. Domestic waste is set aside for recycling. This is a growing trend, providing opportunities for local companies.

Wherever the symbol in Figure 5.1 is shown there will be an involvement with recycling.

Figure 5.1 The international recycling symbol.

Recycling and the disposal of waste materials of all kinds, including toxic and hazardous goods, has become a major new market.

There are several variants:

- the customer-driven approach involving the general public has been a boon for highlighting the possibilities

- non-recyclable waste may be transported to be disposed of at designated sites — this includes hazardous materials and may not be 'proper' recycling but nevertheless provides a large amount of work for logistics operators.

Green logistics

The issue of environmental responsibility has been highlighted in regulatory statutes and in the minds of the consuming public. Regulations to protect the environment have become ever more stringent and environmentally responsible business activity has increased in recent years.

Logistics is a very important component of many environmentally responsible strategies. Logistics managers can affect the success of environmental strategies at each stage of the supply chain.

This is obvious as the managers are involved in decision-making ranging from designing networks, transportation, inventory management, materials handling and purchasing to after-sales and service issues.

Rises in environmentally responsible business activity have included implementation of environmentally responsible logistics.

The global economy requires, if there is to be an integrated approach, policies and practices. The following issues will all be part of discussions and contribute to the final integration of the policies and practices.

As has been alluded to in other parts of the text the environment may not be at the forefront of priorities in the industry but reverse distribution has opened up new market possibilities based on consumer awareness of waste disposal and recycling. Reverse logistics adds to traffic load so at first glance it is difficult to see how transportation companies are becoming 'greener'. 'Greenness' may be imposed by government policies, by the industry or by collaboration between both.

Government intervention sometimes causes difficulties as outcomes can be unpredictable. Issues concerning the greenness of logistics extend beyond transport policies. They include situation of warehouses and terminals and land use. There are many considerations.

Issues relating to planning, operations and

development will help to:

- make sure that logistics infrastructure planning and development integrates short- and long-term economic and environmental considerations

- take a course of action pursuing a direction which is ecologically sustainable and viable, and is conducted according to high standards of environmental performance in order to protect the environment for future generations

- allow for work with community groups, industry stakeholders and government agencies in seeking solutions, and minimising the environmental impacts, associated with infrastructure developments and operations

- make sure that the potential impacts of new projects are identified, assessed on a risk basis and appropriately managed.

Legislative compliance is necessary and will also help logistics operatives to:

- take account of the potential environmental effects of all projects and undertake assessment impacts in accordance with legislative requirements

- comply with all applicable state, territory and national environmental and planning laws and regulations and work with relevant departments and agencies.

Management and use of resources efficiently will help to:

- measure the significant influences and impacts of the logistics operations on the environment using the most appropriate environmental management technologies and practices

- undertake environmental audits / reviews where appropriate to ensure continuing improvement in performance

- use resources efficiently, work to minimise the use of raw materials, toxic substances, energy, water and other resources, encourage the use of new technologies, minimise waste and set up recycling initiatives.

Communications networks:

- are co-operative, share outcomes and communicate openly and honestly with all stakeholders

- encourage broad community and stakeholder involvement in decisions which affect them

- work with staff and contractors who have the appropriate skill and experience, educate, train and motivate them, and ensure full accountability for best environmental practice by all employees and contractors

- ensure awareness of responsible environmental management by staff, customers and the community. Promote research on environmental issues associated with the logistics industry

- have a commitment to continuous improvement of environmental performance and management

- promote of open and effective environmental reporting.

The legislative and regulatory environment globally and nationally will continue to set the standards for the movement of goods and services with government departments working with practitioners to draft workable draft legislation. There is so much legislation now governing the way in which the managers of logistics operations must work. In each country there will be regulation with health and safety advisers working closely with environmentalists.

Activity

 5.4

The following abstract from the UK Health and Safety Executive website (www.hse.gov.uk) helps illustrate (in the area of transportation of dangerous goods in the UK) how safety and environmental issues are part of the overall approach to 'green logistics'.

Read through the extract to familiarise yourself with this framework.

Abstract from Health and Safety Executive

Development of dangerous goods legislation

1. Legislative control of dangerous goods began with the Petroleum Act of 1879 and the Petroleum (Consolidation Act) of 1928. The latter remained (with subsidiary regulations) the major legislative control on the transport of all dangerous substances until the 1980s.

2. Following the introduction of the Health and Safety at Work, etc. Act 1974, proposals were put forward for a single set of regulations, dealing with the classification, packaging and labelling of dangerous substances and regulating the conveyance of dangerous substances by road in tankers, tank containers and packages.

However, when the first consultative document was published in the late 1970s industry made it clear that this was too much to cope with, and it was agreed that the legislation would be divided into three codes:

- The Classification, Labelling and Packaging of Dangerous Substances Regulations 1984 (CPR)

- The Dangerous Substances (Conveyance by Road in Road Tankers and Tank Containers) Regulations 1981 (RTR)

and

- The Dangerous Substances (Conveyance by Road in Packages) Regulations 1986 (PGR).

3. The impact of the 1978 tanker disaster at a campsite in Spain meant that the RTR were given priority and consequently these were introduced ahead of the other regulations.

4. In 1992 RTR and PGR were revoked and replaced by:

- The Road Traffic (Carriage of Dangerous Substances in Packages, etc) Regulations (PGR 92)

and

- The Road Traffic (Carriage of Dangerous Substances in Road Tankers and Tank Containers) Regulations (RTR 92).

5. At the same time new regulations dealing with driver training were introduced:

- The Road Traffic (Training of Drivers of Vehicles Carrying Dangerous Goods) Regulations (DTR).

6. In 1994 the CPR regulations were replaced by:

- The Carriage of Dangerous Goods by Road and Rail (Classification, Packaging and Labelling) Regulations (CDGCPL).

7. In 1996 these were replaced by:

- The Carriage of Dangerous Goods (Classification Packaging and Labelling) and Use of Transportable Pressure Receptacles Regulations

- The Carriage of Dangerous Goods by Road Regulations

- The Carriage of Dangerous Goods by Road (Driver Training) Regulations

- other regulations relating to explosives, radioactive materials and other matters

- ACoPs and guidance were also published.

8. In 1999 various amendments were made but the most significant change was that the Transport of Dangerous Goods (Safety Advisers) Regulations came into force, requiring the appointment of Dangerous Goods Safety Advisers by many duty holders.

Current legislation

9. As a signatory to the European agreement concerning the International Carriage of Dangerous Goods by Road (ADR), and a member state of the EU, the UK is committed to harmonisation of national and international regulations, as far as possible. Therefore, in order to align with the ADR Directives, governing the carriage of dangerous goods by road and rail respectively, a consolidating set of regulations came into force on 10 May 2004.

- The Carriage of Dangerous Goods and Use of Transportable Pressure Equipment Regulations 2004 (SI 2004/568), known in short as the Carriage Regulations

- These regulations were amended in July 2005 mainly to ensure that they refer to the 2005 edition of ADR but also to change some competent authority functions.

10. Apart from radioactive materials, these regulations cover all road and rail carriage of dangerous goods. They directly reference both ADR and RID and provide for some domestic differences (mainly for explosives, but also to retain the UK system of marking road tankers). They also provide some exemptions, for purely domestic transport, that ADR or RID do not.

11. Note that regulation 3 (4) keeps some aspects in scope for radioactive materials. Those most relevant are the need for driver training and appointment of dangerous goods safety advisers.

12. The prescriptive nature of the new regulatory package arises from the need to align domestic legislative arrangements with the ADR and RID codes for the carriage of dangerous goods on international journeys.

Enforcement

13. HSE is the enforcement authority for many aspects of the Carriage Regulations (but note that the Department for Transport is the 'competent authority' for most purposes — see Regulation in paragraph 22 below).

14. HSE has concluded agency agreements to allow suitably appointed police officers and the Vehicle and Operators Standards Agency (VOSA) officers to enforce the regulations 'on the road' (see Operational Strategy and Enforcement). That chapter in the regulations also includes enforcement guidance.

International requirements

15. International standards on the transport of

dangerous goods by road are derived from the recommendations of the UN Committee of Experts. These recommendations are contained in the so-called 'orange book', and form the basis of a series of codes covering the classification, packaging and labelling of dangerous goods for transport by road, rail, sea and air.

16. HSE is mostly involved with the codes for the carriage of dangerous goods by road (ADR) and rail (RID). A code and the technical instructions issued by the International Civil Aviation Organisation (ICAO) deal with the carriage of dangerous goods by sea and air, respectively.

17. The ADR and RID Directives required EU Member States to incorporate the codes into national legislation by 1 January 1997, thereby applying them to domestic as well as international carriage.

18. The international working party on the transport of dangerous goods (WP15), normally meets twice a year to review the conditions governing the international transport of dangerous goods between European countries by road and rail, with the aim of aligning ADR and RID with the UN recommendations. Decisions taken by WP15, when subsequently approved, are included in the latest edition of ADR for implementation. The ADR Code is updated every 2 years.

ADR

19. The ADR agreement allows dangerous goods travelling by road through more than one country to be exempt from the domestic legislation in force in those countries, as long as the requirements of ADR are met in full. However, ADR contains no provisions for enforcement and therefore, where a vehicle travelling under ADR does not comply in full, the vehicle becomes subject to all domestic requirements. As such any enforcement action should be framed in terms of the relevant domestic regulations.

20. In addition, vehicles registered outside the UK may also travel under ADR while carrying dangerous goods on journeys confined to the UK, i.e. on non-international journeys.

This procedure allows for 'cabotage', whereby 'foreign' vehicles may carry dangerous goods on domestic journeys without having to conform to domestic legislation. For example, a Dutch vehicle travelling under ADR on an international journey involving the consignment of dangerous goods from Rotterdam for delivery in Glasgow may pick up another load of dangerous goods in Glasgow for delivery in Hull. Although the Glasgow-Hull journey is not international the vehicle may still travel under ADR.

IMDG

21. The IMDG code contains internationally agreed guidance on the safe transport of dangerous goods by sea, and most commonly relates to the carriage of dangerous goods in freight containers and tank containers. Primarily it is used by shipping operators but it is also relevant to those transporting dangerous goods on journeys involving a sea crossing. In the UK many operators do not undertake complete international journeys but only visit a port to deliver or collect trailers, freight containers or tank containers which have been placarded with IMDG labels for sea journeys.

   Where there is full compliance with the IMDG code, vehicles are exempted from the placarding requirements of the Carriage Regulations. However, all other relevant matters, including training, information in writing, provision of fire-fighting equipment, etc., apply as under the regulations. For the exemptions on placarding to apply, the journey must involve dangerous goods being carried to a port for carriage by sea, or from a port having been carried by sea.

22. Individual countries are responsible for implementing the code under their own legislation and in the UK this is done through The Merchant Shipping (Dangerous Goods and Marine Pollutant) Regulations 1990, which are enforced by the

Department of Transport, and through The Dangerous Substances in Harbour Areas Regulations 1987, as enforced by HSE.

ICAO technical instructions

23. There are analogous provisions in respect of goods packaged and consigned for air transport. Enforcement is by the Civil Aviation Authority (CAA). In this case, ICAO 'technical instructions' set the relevant standards. Details are obviously different but principles are similar. Airlines generally work to IATA rules, which are based on the ICAO technical instructions.

Department for Transport (DfT)

24. DfT is the lead government department on all aspects of transport, in whatever mode, and this includes the transport of dangerous goods by road. Consequently it is the Secretary of State for Transport who responds to Parliament on transport matters.

25. DfT also represents the UK on the various bodies responsible for producing international agreements and standards covering the transport of dangerous substances, i.e. ADR for Road, RID for rail and IMDG for marine.

26. Regulations on the transport of dangerous

substances are made under the Health and Safety at Work etc Act 1974 and are now prepared by DfT. HSE then submits the proposals to the Secretary of State who makes the regulations.

27. DfT takes a close interest in the extent of HSE's activity and, in particular, the number of vehicle checks carried out and level of enforcement. HSE provides the CDG Committee with details of the number of vehicle checks carried out and the extent of enforcement action taken. DfT also collates information from the checklists completed under the terms of the Uniform Monitoring Procedures Directive, and submits an annual report to the EC on levels of enforcement activity within the UK.

28. DfT is the UK competent authority for the certification of packaging. The testing and certification scheme is operated on their behalf by their agents PIRA International. Organisations providing vocational training for drivers of dangerous goods vehicles must be approved by DfT. A list of the current approved training providers may be found on DfT's website.

29. DfT's Radioactive Materials Transport Division (RMTD) enforces the legislation dealing with the carriage of radioactive materials by road.

Liaison arrangements

30. Liaison between DfT, HSE, the police, VOSA and other government departments takes place at the Carriage of Dangerous Goods Committee (CDGC), which meets twice yearly. HID is represented on the Committee by CI4B and SI 2 (Explosives Inspectorate).

CDGC covers all dangerous goods, including radioactive materials and explosives. The transport of radioactive materials is also the subject of a memorandum of understanding between DfT and HSE. HID CI 4 is also represented at HSE/DfT liaison meetings.

31. The police, VOSA and HSE (HID CI 4B) hold a quarterly 'practitioners' forum' where operational problems are discussed. Where needed, CI 4B prepares enforcement guidance in consultation with the practitioners' forum.

32. HSE holds regular meetings with the key trade associations (HSE/Industry Liaison group). DfT and representatives from VOSA and the police and other interested parties are also invited to the meeting.

The illustration provided from the Health and Safety website covers many of the current legislative requirements and collaborative arrangements. UK law is part of the development of health and safety law in the EU and as such constantly evolves. Current issues very much at the forefront are those concerned with the environment.

The logistics industry worldwide has to respond to this type of legislative development. The UK legislation shown in the text will, most likely, mirror legislation throughout the world. There are likely to be differences. Where they exist it is worthwhile looking at the appropriate literature so as to be aware of local requirements. There are issues which will have to be considered regardless of where the organisation is based.

8.6 Current issues concerning green logistics in the logistics industry

Costs

The purpose of logistics is to reduce costs, notably transport costs. In addition, economies of time and improvements in service reliability, including flexibility, are further objectives. Corporations involved in the physical distribution of freight are highly supportive of strategies that enable them to cut transport costs in the present competitive environment.

On some occasions, the cost-saving strategies pursued by logistic operators can be at variance with environmental considerations.

Time

Time is often of the essence. The growth of air freight and trucking is partially the result of time constraints imposed by logistical activities.

The time constraints are themselves the result of an increasing flexibility of industrial production systems and of the retailing sector. Logistics offers door-to-door (DTD) services. Legislation may impact on this.

Reliability

It is impossible to underestimate the importance of service reliability. Its success is based upon the ability to deliver freight on time with the least threat of breakage or damage. Logistics providers often realise these objectives by utilising the modes that are perceived as being most reliable.

The least polluting modes are generally regarded as being the least reliable in terms of on-time delivery, lack of breakage and safety. Ships and railways have inherited a reputation for poor customer satisfaction, and the logistics industry is built around air and truck shipments which are the two least environmentally friendly modes.

Warehousing

Modern logistics systems are based on the reduction of inventories, as the speed and reliability of deliveries removes the need to store and stockpile. Consequently, a reduction in warehousing demands is one of the advantages of logistics.

This means, however, that inventories have been transferred to a certain degree to the transport system, especially the roads. Inventories are actually in transit, contributing still further to congestion and pollution. The environment and society, not the logistical operators, are assuming the external costs.

E-commerce

The distribution activities that have benefited the most from e-commerce are parcel-shipping companies such as UPS and Federal Express that rely solely on trucking and air transportation. Information technologies related to e-commerce applied to logistics can obviously have positive impacts. So once again, the situation may be seen as paradoxical.

It is almost inevitable that there will be further government intervention, for greater environmental regulation, in future years. Local, national, continental and global environmental legislation is already taking hold and it is, in the main, popular. There is some industry resistance to the speed and depth of it and time will tell if this resistance has any foundation in fact.

Individual companies are finding a balance between profit and environmental considerations. It is increasingly acceptable, within the industry, to adopt 'green' policies and measures. Sometimes they can reduce costs but most often the advantages are to do with image and reputation.

Environmental Management Systems such as ISO 14000 may offer opportunities for the green logistics industry.

At the Kyoto conference in December 1997, the world's nations struggled to set binding limits on greenhouse gas emissions to protect future generations. The urgency is often set aside. Even now there is no comprehensive agreement on this issue.

The Kyoto initiative continues to be an issue which is much debated in environmental discussions but it is not possible to determine how far the industrialised nations will go (together) to sign up to the required levels of reductions in emissions.

For the logistics industry the Kyoto issue creates an opportunity to begin research and initiatives to work towards a sustainable transportation system. If nothing else the international debate about what must be done to solve issues such as global warming and carbon emissions has raised the profile of experts' concerns.

Transportation is only one part of the input to global climate change but as it is a growth industry on a global scale any initiatives will have significant impact.

Self-Assessed Question

5.5

Why might it be the case that governments and logistics practitioners disagree about 'green logistics'?

Summary of green logistics

Conscientious consumers, i.e. retailers, market traders and customers, are realising that their actions have social, environmental and ethical consequences. Consumers will increasingly purchase with their conscience.

The issue of global loss of jobs in the industry and the non-unionisation of staff also has impacts. It is not that non-unionisation is necessarily bad where good employers offer staff excellent working conditions.

However, job losses and the potential exploitation of staff by unscrupulous employers continue to be a cause for concern of trade unionists representing people in the industry.

In review of the points made throughout the text the following main points should be kept in mind.

Logistics services have been evolving rapidly in response to changes such as globalisation, general industry re-structure, new production processes and technological advances.

Logistics is broadly defined as the activities needed for the movement and handling of goods and materials, from inputs through production to consumers and waste disposal. It includes reverse flows such as product returns and recycling.

The major logistics activities are transport, storage, procurement, inventory management and packaging. It may be viewed as a set of activities rather than an industry.

Logistics activities are a potential source of competitive advantage for many firms.

Components of performance include:

- cycle times

- on-time delivery

- transit times

- production methods

- delivery options.

The operation and performance of the logistics system is often analysed in terms of chains (e.g. supply chains). A chain is a series of interdependent logistics activities (involving major stages between inputs and disposal) for a particular product. It is based on coordination and cooperation between various logistics service providers (and users of the services).

Effective supply chain management requires integration by combining individual logistics activities into a system that functions seamlessly and provides good performance.

Effective integration within each chain requires:

- proper infrastructure

- adequate information flows

- good co-ordination

- incentives for each provider to promote performance of the whole chain.

Market forces will supply some incentives to co-ordinate activities along and between logistics chains.

There are many issues to watch out for in the next few years, including further technological advances and 'greener' solutions. It is a very interesting time for the industry with no sign of a reversal of the worldwide consumer boom.

8.7 Supply chain issues for the future of international logistics

Most of the key issues have been addressed at different points of the text. Globalisation means that it is no longer possible to operate without knowledge (or access to information) about cross-border and cross-country requirements.

The main issues tend to be as follows.

Concentrating on data interchange and 'greener' logistics, while absolutely essential for the future of the industry, must be tackled alongside the issue of infrastructure and entry/exit points between countries.

Any one logistics company may be using a number of transport gateways to enable the free flow of goods. Ports, road networks, airports and border crossings, for example, are not part of the industry but can cause real problems for the supply chain if there is disruption.

This issue takes on increasing importance as successive governments review transportation policies and, increasingly, pull out of controlling the transportation business.

Private enterprise is taking over; an overview of the UK rail network over the past 20 years gives a good example of how this type of de-nationalisation works.

In raising the awareness of the issue (which is not often considered currently as one of the challenges facing the industry) recent estimates claim that three out of four containers entering the USA do so via ports operated by non-US-owned companies.

This means that the US regulatory authorities are dealing with companies who have headquarters throughout the world.

They are charged with making sure that all ports are managed to comply with US requirements.

There is little media interest in the acquisition of ports, airports, etc. by non-national investors (apart from reports at the time of takeover) but this industry will have to cope with the ever-complex arrangements operating through many gateways owned by several different global operators.

Security issues have become high profile in the past 10 years.

Any traveller going through an airport in the USA cannot help but notice the security checks that are now part of the process of entering that country. This applies at many national airports worldwide and really gives a feel for the seriousness of the need for security measures.

An example of recent changes in gateway security

After the 9/11 incident in the USA the United Nations International Maritime Organisation (IMO) developed the International Ship and Port Facility Security Code (ISCS). This was developed to protect the shipping trade from terrorist attacks.

There may be wide variations in how this code is applied from country to country but it does illustrate the point that, in such a diverse industry, vigilance and change are a constant. The prospect of terrorist threats poses a major problem for the industry.

Just to think of the major impact of targeting passenger airlines or road transport companies carrying abnormal loads gives some idea of the scale of devastation that could happen.

Across the global supply chain workers worldwide who source produce and transport are a vital resource. Representatives of large corporations and representative unions need to work towards equalisation of conditions for people throughout the supply chains.

Reverse logistics will continue to rise in prominence and volume as environmental laws tighten and e-commerce-related returns increase.

Some of the most important recent trends having important implications for future developments can be summarised as:

- smaller, repeated, reliable deliveries

- short order cycles

- variety of delivery patterns

- close partnership relationships

- fewer suppliers

- outsourcing to third parties, allowing for sharing of distribution facilities

- more recycling

- more reverse logistics.

Future developments in EDI systems will undoubtedly depend on how systems are managed.

The issue about the future impact of e-commerce continues to develop.

The trend towards smaller, more frequent deliveries has resulted in more varied patterns of delivery. No one involved in any aspect of logistics can fail to be aware that the industry is continuing to experience the effect of significant changes in a number of key areas.

These include the globalisation of the supply chain, de-regulation and the opening of new markets, combined with the integration of previously separate supply chain activities.

Increased competition is a natural outcome, and customers are demanding shorter delivery times, reductions in costs and improvements to the quality of service.

Furthermore, continuing advances in information and communications technology, the almost universal adoption of the Internet as a business medium and the need to ensure compliance with corporate governance legislation, are also bringing new challenges.

All this has resulted in significant changes in the way companies in the logistics industry operate and interact with their business partners.

More than ever before, logistics businesses are totally reliant on information technology to support the business process, provide ever-improving levels of productivity, facilitate the introduction of new value added services and ensure the ability to maintain a competitive edge.

8.8 Summary of this section

This section has addressed the forces for change impacting on the future development of international logistics.

The main focus has been to accurately explain electronic data systems, assess the impact of reverse logistics in terms of customer needs and correctly assess the need for green logistics.

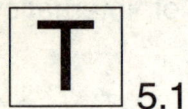

Tutor-marked assignment

Restricted-response questions

1. What are the main advantages to the company of setting up and using EDI?

2. Explain what is meant by the term 'reverse logistics'.

3. How important is the move towards 'green logistics'?

8.9 Answers to SAQs

SAQ 5.1

Companies worldwide rely on electronic data interchange for guaranteed delivery of business transactions. Documentation could include:

- order status reporting

- customs documentation

- customs invoices

- purchase orders

- shipment status

- sales forecasting funds transfer

- warehouse data

- credit transactions

- credit/debit advice

- funds transfer

- schedules

- product updates.

SAQ 5.2

You may have defined it as 'the exchange of business data from one organisation's computer application to the computer application of a trading organisation' or something similar.

SAQ 5.3

It is more than just the issue of moving data from one point to another when the information is exchanged over the Internet.

Most business documents exchanged over the Internet will include sensitive information, e.g. sales figures, warehouse inventories, etc. Businesses require that this information is transferred quickly, securely and reliably. It is therefore necessary to have systems in place that ensure this.

SAQ 5.4

They can improve processes by making employees aware of the significance. The same applies to suppliers, sellers and customers.

Many of the good practices of forward logistics can be

applied to reverse logistics, e.g. adequate allocation of resources, adequate administrative systems and tracking systems.

SAQ 5.5

A difficulty with government intervention is that the outcomes are often unpredictable, and in an industry as complex as logistics, many could be unexpected and unwanted.

Environmentally-inspired policies may impact on freight and passenger traffic differentially, just as different modes may experience widely variable results of a common regulation. Issues concerning the greenness of logistics extend beyond transport regulations.

The siting of terminals and warehouses are crucial to moving the industry towards the goal of sustainability, yet these are often under the land use and zoning control of lower levels of government whose environmental interests may be at variance with national and international bodies.

8.10 Answers to activities

Activity 5.1

1. Advantages:

   - Eliminates VAN costs

   - Fast and reliable connections

   - Digital signatures can ensure authenticity

   - Document alteration during transmission can be detected.

2. Disadvantages

   - Costs of software very high

   - Only works on some networks, i.e. over TCP/IP networks

   - Investment returns will only apply if there are volume connections

   - Management of certificates used for secure connections

   - Data cannot be pulled

   - No file restart facility.

3. Yes there are other protocols, e.g. ISDN and X.25.

4. Exchange of data over the Internet involves more than moving data from one point to another. Business documents exchanged over the Internet may contain sensitive material, for example sales figures, and these must be transferred securely, reliably and quickly. AS2 allows such information to be sent over public and private global networks to be digitally signed and secured.

Activity 5.2

There will be no one definitive response.

Recalls mentioned might include:

- In 2006 Sony notebook batteries were recalled (sparking recall of many other brand batteries).

- In 2003, in Australia, Pan Pharmaceuticals recalled several goods after failing quality standards tests.

- In 2005, in the UK and Canada, potentially carcinogenic food colour found in 400 products containing Worcester sauce were recalled.

- In 2000, in the USA, the Ford Motor Company recalled 6.5 million 15-inch Firestone tyres.

Activity 5.3

Some materials that can be recycled are:

- glass

- plastic

- paper

- tin

- aluminium

- fabrics

- iron.

These are just a few examples.

Activity 5.4

There is no specific answer to this activity.

9 Glossary

Carrier	Company accepting responsibility for the transport of goods for delivery.
Consumables	For consumer use, e.g. fuel, foodstuffs.
Discount stores	Self-service stores selling a limited range of goods, often recalls.
EDI	Electronic data interchange.
Finished goods	Goods ready for sale.
Freight forwarder	Company that arranges goods transport on behalf of another.
Goal	An ideal situation to be achieved.
Inter-modal	The use of one mode of transport during a single door-to-door delivery.
Logistics	Management of flow of materials information and money in a way that allows raw materials to be transformed into finished products.
Multi-modal	The use of more than one mode of transport during a single door-to-door delivery.
Operational management	Day-to-day activities.
Outsource	Give out work to specialist provider.
Partnerships	Business carried on between two or more people sharing ownership.
Primary activities	The manufacture and sale of basic materials.

Retailing	The sale of goods to individual consumers.
Reverse logistics	Process for recall/recycling of merchandise.
Secondary activities	Manufacture of capital and intermediate goods.
Third party logistics	Company which manages on behalf of others, the flow of materials, information and money associated with the manufacture and distribution of goods.
Shareholder	A person who owns a share in a limited company.
Stock	Goods held for resale in the normal course of business.
Stock control	Tracking how much stock there is and how it is tracked.
Strategic management	Long-term forward planning.
Syntax	Use of language.
Transport infrastructure	Immobile fixed assets involved in the production of transport services.
Transport policy	Process of defining measures within the transport sector to achieve societal goals.
Transport services	Movement of passengers or goods.
VAN	Value added network.
Work in progress	Stocks of unfinished goods.
Wholesaling	Sale of goods by companies other than the manufacturer to companies intending to sell the goods to consumers.
XML	Extensible mark-up language.

10 Acknowledgements

SQA gratefully acknowledges the contributions made by Scotland's colleges in the authoring, editing and publishing of this material.

Every effort has been made to trace copyright holders but if any have been inadvertently overlooked the publishers (Scottish Qualifications Authority) will be pleased to make the necessary arrangements at the first opportunity.

Any material sourced is referenced.

著作权合同登记　图字：01-2008-3354号
图书在版编目(CIP)数据

国际物流：英文／苏格兰学历管理委员会著．
—北京：中国时代经济出版社，2010.5（2014.7重印）
ISBN 978-7-80221-445-3

Ⅰ．国… Ⅱ．苏… Ⅲ．国际贸易-物流-高等学校-教材-英文
Ⅳ．F252

中国版本图书馆CIP数据核字(2007)第135151号

"First published by CMEPH"
"All Rights Reserved"
"Authorized Apograph/Translation/Adaptation of the editions by the Scottish Qualifications Authority. All Intellectual Property Rights vest in the Scottish Qualifications Authority and no part of these "Works" may be reproduced in any form without the express written permission of Scottish Qualifications Authority"

书　　名：	国际物流
作　　者：	苏格兰学历管理委员会
出版发行：	中国时代经济出版社
社　　址：	北京市丰台区右安门外玉林里25号
邮政编码：	100069
发行热线：	(010)68320825　88361317
传　　真：	(010)68320634　68320697
网　　址：	www.cmepub.com.cn
电子邮箱：	zgsdjj@hotmail.com
经　　销：	各地新华书店
印　　刷：	北京昌平百善印刷厂
开　　本：	787×1092　1/16
字　　数：	235千字
印　　张：	19.75
版　　次：	2007年9月第1版
印　　次：	2014年7月第6次印刷
书　　号：	ISBN 978-7-80221-445-3
定　　价：	59.00元

本书如有破损、缺页、装订错误，请与本社发行部联系更换
版权所有　侵权必究